HELP!

I'M TURNING

INTO MY

MUM!

This edition published in 2011

First published in 2008 by Prion
An imprint of
Carlton Books Limited
20 Mortimer Street
London W1T 3JW

Text © 2008 Carlton Books Limited
Design © 2008 Carlton Books Limited

A catalogue record for this book is available
from the British Library

ISBN: 978-1-85375-822-5

Printed in the UK by CPI Group (UK), Croydon, CR0 4YY

HELP!

I'M TURNING INTO MY MUM!

A GUIDE TO COPING WITH THE PERILS OF MIDDLE AGE

GINA McKINNON

WITH CARTOONS BY
MIKE MOSEDALE

PRION

Contents

Introduction

Noticed anything different about yourself lately? Have you started ironing sheets, tea towels and your – increasingly sensible – pants? Have you swapped the pub for a trug; parties for weeding, breeding and reading? Have gardening, babies and books swallowed your social life whole? Could you, if truth be told, be turning into your Mum?

Fear not! You're not alone. Flick through the pages of this book and you'll find all manner of behaviour which points to that terrible time in every woman's life when she looks into the mirror and sees her mother staring back at her. Worse yet, she's nodding sagely, "Told you so!"

In our youth, we swore we would never ever be like our mothers. But suddenly the words, "You treat this house like a hotel!" … "Am I talking to a brick wall?" … "Money doesn't grow on trees," or other such classic Mum sayings escape our lips and we cringe at the realization that the inevitable process has begun. Down at the shops or the allotment (where we spend an increasing amount of time), or at the kitchen sink (ditto), the golden nuggets of Mum's good old-fashioned advice come flooding back with unwelcome spontaneity.

Don't worry, there's no shame in joining the legions of women who are on the rocky road to Mum-land. Women who, for instance, once let their hair down and would now do anything but. For one thing there's no hair to let down as once-flowing locks have been cut into a nice, sensible bob, or Princess Di crop. So much more manageable like that, wouldn't your dear Mama have said? For another, politics and parenting, not partying, have become their number one priority, the main topic of conversation when they are out (or rather in – they don't get out much these days) with the girls. Girls just want to have fun, and Mums most definitely don't!

Up and down the land previously sane and sassy women are turning into their Mums. Just like you (and her) they're becoming spartan where they once were spendthrifts; they plan dinner parties, birthdays and Xmas with almost military precision; and hoover before breakfast, "just to get things straight." These women need help and if you are one of them, then so do you.

So, why not settle down with a glass of sherry, put on your comfiest cardie and try and come to terms with the embarrassingly familiar scenarios, the cringe-making confessions and awkward mumsy moments you will find in the pages of this book.

There, you feel better already!

Chapter 1

Culture Vulture

Let's start by going in at the deep end, with a look at an area which should leave you in no doubt whatsoever that you are taking the unavoidable plunge into middle age and replicating the actions and achievements of previous generations. The subject of our no-holds barred look at your impending transformation is one which guarantees at least a glimmer (or maybe a grimace) of recognition about your waning love affair with pop culture, and your increasing interest in the "highbrow" stuff.

"Last week we paid £400 for a box at Covent Garden to see *Il Barbiere Di Siviglia* and I spent the entire performance daydreaming of *Take That*."

Culture was not a word that often passed your lips in adolescence – apart from when you were referring to Boy George and co, perhaps. As you reached your 20s and enjoyed that technically adult yet fundamentally immature period that has come to be known as "kidulthood", things did not get much better. You might have visited the odd exhibition, seen the occasional play, picked up a book every now and then, but high culture was still something you associated with exams.

At the same time you had an enormous appetite for the less sophisticated side of the coin: popular culture. You gobbled up the latest trendy movies, CDs and novels, only to discard them weeks later for the next "in" thing. Even if you didn't take much interest in the pop charts, you always knew who was Number One by the same sort of weird youthful osmosis which alerted you on the *exact* day that stone-washed jeans went out of fashion. (FYI, they went out some time ago... just in case!)

However, as you make the leap from kidulthood to fully fledged adulthood, your finger could hardly be said to be on the pulse any longer. In fact it's so far from the pulse, you're not sure what the pulse actually is. Of course the amount of time you spend watching hospital dramas should give you *some* inkling, but this is sadly yet one more indication that you are no longer "down with the kids".

Who could blame you? Being "down" and keeping up with the latest trends is quite simply exhausting and doesn't fit in at all with your new priorities of comfy seating, easy parking and an early night. Something a little more refined, a little more sedate is definitely in order.

FACING THE MUSIC

The first victim to fall at the hands of your need for a sedentary life is your taste in music. If we were going to get all Shakespearean (Oh goody! Nothing you like more at present than a bit of the Bard) we'd talk about music being the food of love. And if we did, we wouldn't go far wrong if we said that in the past you listened to the equivalent of a meat pie or burger and chips – quite appropriate really, for this is what you munched on after shaking your bootie for 10 hours solid at some music festival or other. Pop, rock or dance music might have been your sonic sensations of choice. Nowadays your tastes – in so many ways – are much more superior and we could compare your musical preference to lobster – or at the very least gamberetti. All right, I know you're not quite at the easy listening stage just yet, but do feel free to admit you prefer something a little easier on the ear than death metal or banging techno.

The criterion you employed in the past for who-was-hot-and-who-was-not was about image as much as musicality. And we're talking about image here in two ways: theirs and yours. Theirs, in that you didn't really like the dulcet tones of *Take That* or Robbie Williams *that* much but it was a convenient excuse for lusting after them – even at the should-know-better age of 25! As for *your* image, you listened to the melancholically pained strains of indie bands with an outer fervour not quite matching your inner apathy – deep down you thought they sucked but you didn't want the "in-crowd" to know you preferred jazz or folk music!

Then there came a time, as sure as eggs is eggs, and as sure is Morrissey is probably quite a happy chap *really*, when you thought: "Hmm, I'm not sure listening to *Teenage Fanclub* or flipping out to *Teenage Kicks* is befitting of someone whose 30th birthday party is an increasingly distant memory." It would be fair to say that it's a pretty sure sign that you are becoming like your Mum when you decide to stop listening to such wannabe adolescent warblings, and it's time to diagnose you with full-blown "Mumitis" when you even stop pretending that you do!

As for the aforementioned *Take That*, when bands like these and the *Spice Girls* made a comeback, instead of being delighted that the idols of your youth were coming back into style you grumbled, "I mean, really, weren't they so much better the first time around?" Instead of listening to their latest offering, you cosy up to their golden oldies on a compilation CD that might as well be called *Help! I'm Turning into My Mum!* Quick, get thee down to Woolies, where the shelves are fair groaning with other similar such crappy compilations.

MUM ROCK

"But not so fast," you cry. "There's life in the old dog yet! I still go and watch live gigs." Sure you do, but why is it that as our age increases, so does the size of the concert venue we attend? In the past you'd have gone to any sleazy little bar, dive or club. You loved nothing more than to inhale dry ice and smoke, and if you didn't come home smelling of fags, beer and possibly vomit, well, it just wasn't a good night, was it?

Now you decide that bigger is better and drive insanely long distances to listen to bands you don't even like that much anymore – but at least at open-air or enormous gigs you can breathe nice clean, fresh air! There's something about an enormo-gig in the grounds of a stately home, isn't there? If the weather's good, you can break out a picnic (white wine, home-made sandwiches; no rip-off drinks from the bar for you!). If it's bad, there's a wonderful opportunity to smugly don your favourite waterproofs with the same satisfaction you previously enjoyed wearing a band T-shirt. The parking is ample, the volume low, and it will all be over by 10.30pm at the latest! Marvellous!

Marvellous? Really? You may as well confess that you get dragged along to such lame gigs reluctantly – you're among like-minded losers here! In fact, if you had your way, you'd happily just sit at home tapping your foot along to Radio 2!

What makes you think anyone would miss you, anyway? While we're being truthful, there's no harm in revealing that at such gigs you might well be mistaken for the Invisible Woman. I mean, it's fair to say you're no longer the girl in the front row riding on her boyfriend's shoulders (well, poor love, he *has* only just recovered from that slipped disk) or the one to be picked out by the band to dance with them on stage. We're more likely to find you in the kitchen mashing potatoes than moshing; and the only stage you set foot on is at the local amateur dramatics society. (Gilbert and Sullivan, Shakespeare anybody?) Altogether now: "Three little maids from school are we!"

"Are they actually playing or has my tinnitus
started up again ?"

But there's one time when you do get noticed at such events, when the crowd do sit up and take notice – and, I hate to say, for all the wrong reasons – and that's when you start Mum Dancing. Sure it was "cool" to jitter-bug in the 80s or pack boxes and make shapes in the air in the 90s but we're in the noughties now, lady, so settle down and stop showing yourself up!

BROADCAST BLUES

So, you make the long, sober drive home, asking yourself whether it was all worth it and decide it'll be preferable to stay at home next time and watch a repeat of *Inspector Morse* on the telly. Dearie me. Just the sort of night's viewing that, um, switches your Mum on, eh?

Indeed, what you watch on the box provides us with further evidence that you are beginning to conform to her idea of what's poptastic and what's *passé*. So, it's goodbye Channel 4, spending Sunday lolling around watching pop videos, comedy programmes and soap omnibuses in the hope that simply by so doing you'll stay young and hip! In fact, you shudder to think how many hungover hours you spent absorbing trash TV, and look back on those days as your dumbed-down decade.

For you have now discovered what a wealth of knowledge and information TV actually provides! And so, your love affair with the History and Discovery channels begins. Well I never! Never before had you realized how fascinating Adolf Hitler's love life could be, how captivating the beauty of the Amazonian rainforest or how absorbing the sex life of the stingray. Never before had you... been so like your Mum! Suddenly "thought-provoking" is the highest term of praise you can bestow on a programme. Whatever happened to "riveting" or even "sexy"? Nope, what you need is a nice steady stream of information. As such, you never miss *News at Ten* or *Newsnight*, and you positively salivate if you know Germaine Greer is set to appear on one of those late-night culture shows! Newsflash: this kind of behaviour is not going to slow down your journey to hell in a handcart!

"You're right.....it is more thought provoking."

You'd be lying if you said you've given up on soap operas and the like completely, but for some time now you've found *Corrie* and *EastEnders* as intellectually challenging as watching an empty cardboard box. So, you switch to a more erudite and grown-up soap such as *The Sopranos*. No chance your Mum will call up to interrupt your TV pleasure while that show's on – she'll no doubt be glued to her set as well!

Even your approach to watching telly is making your Mumological clock tick that bit faster (like a biological one but even crueler). No longer do you slump contentedly in front of the box for hours, channel-hopping without even blinking. These days the most cringe-and-noteworthy tele-visual signal that you are becoming more like your Mum is when you not only buy the *Radio Times*, but catch yourself circling the programmes you want to watch, as you now plan your TV viewing a week in advance.

SUN, SEA AND...SOPHISTICATION

Unfortunately it gets worse: if you're not watching pseudo-academic documentaries about the history of ancient ruins on TV, such is your proclivity toward pre-history, you excitedly plan visits to the actual location of said programmes on your annual vacation. Oh! Oh! I can almost hear the horrified yells of your kids and partner from here. Do you really intend to drag them on a quest to find the ancient city of Atlantis on your one foreign holiday a year? Or worse yet, on a blustery walking tour of Finland? In November?

Of course you do! For – like the kings and queens who so fascinate you – your love of the relaxing beach holiday is dead and buried.

Not that you exactly relaxed on those boozy beach holidays of times gone by. *Au contraire*: the wild vacations of your salad days were a hedonistic marathon of sun, sea and... well, you know! Spending 10 days drinking as much as possible, while wearing as little as possible, was your idea of heaven, and if the resort wasn't chock-a-block with chips and cheeky chappies, you'd have whinged, "Money back!"

A more recent brochure for your ideal holiday might read: "Come to Spain/France/Portugal [delete resort as appropriate] and discover a world of culture and history. Spend a fortnight driving your family potty as you fill your days with "edutainment"; waste hours searching for the "real" Malaga/Torremolinos/Athens (or to put it another, more realistic, way: getting lost) and eat only local specialities and wines." Rabbit's foot stew or spicy sea-slug special, anybody?

Mind you, it would be stretching the truth somewhat to say that you go in for the exotic *that much*, as nine times out of 10 it's likely you choose self-catering, just to feel more at home!

Choosing this arrangement over an all-inclusive holiday is evidence that, just like your Mum, you have forgotten that true definition of a holiday, which is widely accepted to be "take time off and relax". Instead you keep yourself busy, hand-washing swimwear and towels, making sure everyone is smothered in impenetrable layers of sunblock, and – last but not least – donning your archaeologist's hat, digging into the history of the local area with vim and vigour.

A favoured area for this new-found love of exploration is the church or cathedral. Even if you have not set foot in a place of worship (unless you count aforementioned *Take That* concerts) in your home country since your schooldays – or especially if you have – the local church becomes a must-see feature of your holiday. Well, at least they're usually cool... "What is it about the bloody continent," you're sure to be found moaning, "that makes it so bloody HOT?" (This comment is conventionally followed by "Not that I've got a problem with the heat, it's the HUMIDITY that makes it so darned sticky!")

"There... if we'd paid out for sunloungers on holiday we'd never have been able to afford this authentic bedstead."

Get you, digging deep into the past! Sadly this is the only thing you will dig deep into on your holibops as holiday time is certain to bring out the mumsy miser in you. When the family do finally manage to drag you to the beach, you are to be found thundering, "Ten euros for a sun-lounger? I'll take my chances on the shingle!" Despite pester power from all and sundry, the only time you spare no expense is to purchase a "stunningly hand-crafted" local Spanish artefact that would sit so nicely on the mantelpiece at home.

Unfortunately, when you do finally escape foreign climes and find your way back to dear old Blighty, you find "Made in China" stamped on the bottom! Some culture vulture you are!

MAKING A DAY OF IT

Better to say closer to home, really... Though you can be sure as Betsy, if you do, you won't moan any less about the cost of high days and holidays in "Rip-off Britain!" Not quite what Prince Albert intended when he dreamt up the Great Exhibition of 1851. This exhibition held in London's Crystal Palace was Britain's crowning glory as world leader of the Industrial Revolution. (Trust me, I'm going some-where with this.) For the first time in history, by virtue of the newly built railways, people from all backgrounds were able to gather together in large numbers.

Had Prince Albert known that this event would be the catalyst for future near-death experiences on the M25, meals so grim they'd put the gruel of his wife's workhouses to shame and hordes of young children driving their parents mental, crying, "Are we there yet?", him and his fellow exhibitioners might have stayed in bed that day. Yes, I'm blaming him and his cronies for that weekly, monthly or annual event (depending on how brave or madly desperate you are) we all know and dread: The Family Day Out.

"Hello 'Childline'.... my parents just don't rock."

Why is it that budding Mums and Dads everywhere inflict this horror-ful occasion on their own flesh and blood, as if making them spend their holidays on archaeological digs wasn't cruel enough?

If kids had their way, The Family Day Out would be a no-brainer. Why go to the trouble of looking into an alternative when places such as Alton Towers, Blackpool Pleasure Beach or Chessington World of Adventures hand fun to you on a plate? But "no-brainers" or "fun" aren't in your vocabulary these days, are they? Instead you insist that The Family Day Out should be educational, stimulating, rewarding or – if we translated this back into the language of the little people – "boring!"

Where to go to tick all of the above boxes? Why, to the local museum or art gallery, of course! Never mind that you've paid a visit there nigh on every wet weekend for the last few years. Come on, surely you can think of somewhere further afield? Well, yes, of course you can. You just knew that the National Trust membership you bought your husband for Christmas would come in handy during the summer holidays!

A ramble around a country garden, nosing about a stately home (and without the additional nuisance of listening to some ageing crooner!), a nice cup of tea and a slice of cake. Bliss! You're well on your way to earning your stripes as Mum when you organize such outings – and you're a fully paid-up member of the Mum gang when you invite your friends to join you on such days out, with no apology made for the un-rock-'n'-roll-ness of it.

Not that you care. You've completely abandoned hope of ever being hip and trendy again, and "chill out" with no shame or embarrassment to Enya's *Orinoco Flow* in the bath. So, you rejoice rather than rue the day when you take a deep breath and re-programme your car stereo or digital radio to Radio 2 and Classic FM. What's more, when you are giving your best friend a lift, it's not like you quickly tune back in to Radio 1, or make a feeble excuse for the easy-listening option. You simply sigh: "Gosh, Radio 1 is simply a NOISE these days," and she nods approvingly back at you.

Chapter 2

Green Goddesses

Have you developed a love for the Great Outdoors recently? Do you find that, as the kids' and your partner's stuff accumulates indoors, you've acquired an increasingly overwhelming urge to flee into the fresh, open air, and make your vista more verdant? Have you abandoned clubs and pubs for shrubs and trugs, having discovered the classically middle-aged weekend pursuit of gardening?

Course you have. Gone are the days when you could spend hours at home, specifically in bed, rolling around in your own dirt, happy as a pig in you know what. Think back to the bedroom of your adolescence: curtains drawn to keep out daylight; the only plant or wild-life that existed was the mould growing on top of the dozens of half-empty coffee mugs dotted around the room; window closed even in high summer to get maximum festering points from your mates.

Things didn't improve much in your twenties. Sure, you might have stepped outdoors a bit more often, gone to the occasional country retreat. But the country retreat was probably somewhere you went during many a "dirty weekend", so it's unlikely you saw much more than the four walls (or the ceiling) of your country hotel room.

Currently you like nothing better than the wind in your face – the icier and chillier, the better. You crave a life in the country, but if this isn't possible you more than make do with your back garden or allotment. If you were a comic-book character you would be "The Green Goddess", whose super-power would be an empathic bond with nature, and with an innate impulse to dig, plant and weed.

"I grow all our tomatoes. I grow all our spinach. All you do is complain about the cost of my twice-weekly manicures."

EVERYTHING'S COMING UP ROSES

And why not, you might say? There's nothing like spending time in the garden to brush off the cobwebs, toiling away the stress and worries of the day. Gardening is a wonderful tool for relaxation: the physical effort involved; the sense of satisfaction and reward one feels to see months of careful planning blossom into a riot of colour; the almost spiritual wonder of getting back to nature – even if you only have a 2ft square courtyard and a titchy urban flat.

Still, not really a young person's game, is it? The only time we'll find our friends under 30 pulling weeds is when they fall for a scrawny geeky type down the pub. As for topiary, well, the younger generation seems very much concerned with trimming "down-below" but that's about as far as it goes... Consider your own youth. Surely the closest you came to being green-fingered was that time you drunkenly painted your student flat the colours of the Rasta flag. More to the point, back then the only plants anyone you knew cultivated were of the kind smoked by your aforementioned Rastafarian friends.

Yet now you dig, sow and plant all manner of blooms and blossoms, and have a love of gardening in spades! (Spades, do you see? Boom! Boom!) Like other women up and down the country suffering from pre-mid-life crises, you spend an inordinate amount of time weeding, seeding and feeding – when you are not to be found breeding and reading, that is. I'm afraid this means if we had to identify you for a nature encyclopaedia, if we had to come up with a new breed of human being to describe your

27

botanically obsessed behaviour, there would only be one accurate definition: the common-or-garden Mum!

The Mum gardener differs from other amateur horticulturalists in one significant way. The summer months are typically considered the highlight of the gardener's calendar, as the garden becomes resplendent with the fruits, quite literally, of their labour. Green foliage and shrubbery is abundant and evident for all to see, and a cornucopia of flowers are in full bloom with bees buzzing happily around the Eden you have created.

No such pleasure is taken in this heavenly setting by Mum gardeners, though. Hmm, I wonder why this is? Just why is it that she conversely spends less time in the garden in the summer months, in daylight hours at least? Here, I'll give you a clue: it's in the warmest season that the garden comes into its own as that one extra room in the house. Dad, for instance, becomes obsessed by keeping the lawn mowed at that perfect half-inch height, the kids wail constantly for you to fill the paddling pool, and any teens you may have sullenly hog the sun-lounger with the portable radio tuned to Radio 1. Or, worse still, 1 Xtra!

Small wonder that you snub your horticultural haven when you should be most appreciative of it! Not that you give up on the garden completely. As we've said you only snub your shrubs in daylight hours. But you are sure to be found on those balmy warm summer evenings, watering and weeding while everyone else is safely tucked up in bed or tucking into supper, requisite glass of wine in one hand, trowel in the other.

"Not again... new plug, new filter and it still
won't bloody well start."

Indeed, your nocturnal capers suggest that your gardening obsession is undiminished during the summer season. Quite the reverse actually. But you transport your obsession away from home, so the minute the Great British Summertime begins and the sun peeps out from behind the clouds, as you hear the thud of the summer

29

paraphernalia being dragged out of cupboards, you jump in the car and shout, "Just off to the gardening centre!"

What bliss! What joy! Even though your private space has been invaded you can indulge your horticultural hobby as you mooch about the gardening centre eyeing up terracotta pots, trellises and the like. You've taken a notebook, you've taken a handbook, you're poking under leaves to check for white fly, green fly and black fly. You're quite happy that you'll be here for over an hour before you even think of *buying* anything. But look, that woman over there is about to pounce on the last cut-price herb garden. No way José, you spotted it first! But isn't there something strangely familiar about the paisley-patterned cardigan she's wearing? Who cares? you think, as you cut a mad dash across the herbaceous borders. Recognize her yet? Sure you do. It's your Mum!

And as you tussle, laughing, over said herb garden, you decide the game is up: there is no doubt in your mind you are turning into her. So, with a resigned giggle, you suggest a visit to the local stately home to visit its boundless and beautiful gardens... (Breathing a huge sigh of relief that there aren't any rock concerts scheduled for that evening – you've given up on them, remember?)

The problem is, the minute you arrive there, you realize you were plain daft to question whether history was repeating itself, as you unconsciously begin another maternal baptism of fire. Even though it made you squeal with embarrassment as a child, you reach in your handbag for the secateurs and take a cutting for your back garden.

LOSING THE PLOT

As you put the key in the lock on the return home you hope to hear all hell breaking loose indoors, meaning you can plant your cutting immediately in the tranquillity of your outdoor sanctuary. Tough luck! It's an Indian summer so you'll have to wait a month or two for that solitary pleasure. Suddenly, frustration. Your lovingly tended oasis has been occupied by your lovingly tended brood. Your dream of sharing it with the birds and bees has been shattered by having to share it with those you supposedly love the most.

Where can you find the sacred space you deserve, where no-one will encroach on your, err, turf, and where it's just you, the plants and the pollen? Then it comes to you quick as a flash! "Why, I need an allotment!" And so you begin a fantasy of toiling away to your (artichoke) heart's content without any interruption from annoying family members. You don't need me to tell you that the woman whose fantasies about wild men have been replaced by an almost sexual fervour for wild flowers and veg – the woman who begins to fetishize the ordinary vegetable – is without doubt turning into her Mum.

In the past you might have put your name down on a waiting list to get entry to a trendy members' club and bar. You crossed everything, hoping that you would be cool enough to get in, or that snogging the bouncer would speed up your application. As we bring things up-to-date, you only have one burning desire, your name is only down on one list, for something so competitive that you almost wonder if it's controlled by the local mafia.

And that's an allotment space! Why did her next door get her patch after only a six-month wait, you fume – she must be sleeping with somebody from the council...

And the conspiracy theories and rivalry don't stop once the glorious day arrives and your plotting to secure your, ahem, plot comes off. Oh no! It's only just begun. Granted, for the first few days or weeks you chit-chat with your neighbouring allotment-eer, hanging over the dividing fence, discussing weather patterns, crop rotations and the like. Get you and your propagation conversation!

But the allotment soon becomes fertile ground for a rivalry more competitive than even the most sororicidal siblings have ever known. Hmm, why did their Brussels turn out in abundance while mine were blighted by slugs? Why are her tomatoes as big as tennis balls while mine resemble withered red nipples? And how come they've got sodding time to dig and tend to a pond at the bottom of their plot? As for your friends with allotments, you now compete over who has produced the biggest carrot – a far cry from the days when you competed over whose boyfriend had the biggest, um, let's be decent about this, carrot-shaped thing!

So, when friends come over for dinner, you rustle up a little something which has home-grown written all over it. Just what is it about slipping from the circle of life's equivalent of a seedling to shedding plant that makes us so blinking precious about the food that we eat? Nothing says middle age more than spurning the chicken nugget or a good old-fashioned plate of fish and chips. Now you measure how nice a meal is not by how good it tastes, but how much of it has been dug up by your own fair, dirty fingernailed hand. So what if they cry, "Mum, I've found a worm in my dinner!" Good, you think, no pesky pesticides in this household.

It would also be fair to say that if you've not grown the food yourself, then the consolation prize is that it has to be "in season", locally produced or from a farmer's market. Quite how you'll marry this up with your love of the cheap supermarket, God only knows, but as your Mum always said, "Where there's a will, there's a way!"

Although a visit to the farmer's market isn't always what it's cracked up to be. (No! Really?) Things can turn pretty nasty as you turn quite green with envy over the farmer's, um, greens – after all that effort you put into the spinach, yours is stringy, floppy, full of sinister bite-sized holes and not fit even for Popeye!

THE CALL OF THE WILD

Still, you're becoming quite the skilled amateur farmer, gardener and botanist, aren't you dear? But to your mind, nothing quite beats the real thing, and that's getting back to nature and being eye witness to the flora and fauna of the Great Outdoors. It's as if whoever put us here inserted a magic button that switches us onto nature the minute the ageing process speeds up and our number of birthdays increases.

As you peer over this precipice of middle age "the call of the wild" is no longer that magnetic attraction you have for wild nights out and unmanageable men but, rather, the lure of the natural world; and it's not your men you like rough and rugged – but the landscapes you attempt to traverse on your many walks in the country. Forgetting that you whined and moaned when your own Mum suggested the very same, you encourage your kith and kin to join you on long rambles through the brambles, roaming in the gloaming and other such country ways. As you speak the words, "Don't you just love all that lovely fresh country air?" Either somebody's playing a recording of your mother's voice or you're starting to sound just like her.

"Mush!"

The bleaker, the wilder, the less accessible the terrain, the happier you are. For some reason, known only to you and your Mum, as you turn into her, you decide that using maps is for squares, and that off the beaten track is so much more fun! Never mind that you have a couple of toddlers in tow, one of whom isn't potty-trained. Nothing like having a dump outside to feel at one with Mother Nature. And should the teenagers whine that they'd rather be home, making contact with the real world (on some social networking site – oh the irony!), you mutter, "You'll look back and appreciate this healthy lifestyle when you're older!" Or, in other words, "You'll be able to get revenge on life by inflicting these tortuous treks on your own kids when you're older, so button it!"

Fair play to you: you've packed your wind cheater, your sensible walking boots and your all-weather waterproof coat – all good clean, *dry*, fun for you then. So, as it starts to rain cats and dogs and the rest of the family are turned out in inappropriate apparel you gloat, "Who's laughing, who's the anorak now?" Then, as you realize that the wet stuff on the face of your first born is not splashes of good, healthy rain, but tears of frustration, and that their teeth aren't chattering because they're chewing gum, you get a healthy dose of the guilts and make a mental note: wind-cheaters all around next Xmas!

Of course, if we looked back at your own past, we'd discover you used to be more a nature fighter than a nature lover. The closest you came to England's green and pleasant land was when you hung about in the park or the school playing fields drinking Thunderbird double-strength wine.

You might have gone on bike rides to the local countryside, but that was only so you could be as far away as possible from the local arm of the law for whatever reason.

"I see you've been talking to the plants again."

As you pass your 30th birthday, it's as if your brain has been magically filled with the wonder of nature and you gain an almost encyclopaedic knowledge of every breed of bird or flower. Dr Doolittle has got nothing on you! You can count ornithology, botany and zoology among your favourite pastimes. Quite the big change from the days when you ran a mile from any word with 'ology' on the end, fearing it was all a bit too intellectual for your befuddled young brain.

Mind you, you can't be outdoors all the time, can you? "What to do?" you panic. "I literally can't breathe without good clean air around me." What to do? Why, fill your home with a veritable jungle of houseplants and cut flowers of course. Indeed, believing that we are all going to die of the radiation emanating from the spoils of modern life, the woman who turns into her Mum, buys a different breed of houseplant to place next to each electrical appliance in the house. And the woman who clearly is her Mum takes it one step further and talks to said plants more than she does her kids!

As you obsess more and more about the environment and about your carbon footprint, you decide what the world needs is more trees. You therefore buy everyone you know tree gifts every birthday, Christmas and anniversary. Well, we've only got one planet, you think to yourself, and you'll do all you can to stop it from being destroyed. Hence plastic bags, cars and aeroplanes are out, cotton fabric shoppers, walking and cycling are in.

In fact, with these trappings of the modern world ditched, as you sacrifice modern luxuries for old-fashioned hardship, you seem to be transporting yourself back to a more supposedly greener time. Back to the 1950s...

Back in fact, to the formative years of you-know-who!

Years when mothers everywhere brought up their children to know the difference between a chaffinch and a bullfinch, between a filly and a foal, and between poisonous fungi or edible mushrooms. A time when Enid Blyton's *Nature Lover's Guide* came second only to *The Bible* on the family's bookshelves. Hmm, never mind that the post-war parent chain-smoked indoors in good conscience, or that the advent of modern household appliances was the beginning of the end for our natural resources, or indeed that factories pumped out cloud after poisonous cloud of pollution: they're your rose-tinted spectacles and you'll wear them as often as you like, thank you very much. Oh, for the environmentally unfriendly times of your Mum!

Chapter 3

Men! Huh! What Are They Good For?

Once upon a time there lived a young woman who daydreamed about her Mr Right, the ideal man who would charge forth on his white steed (or if the lady in question was more realistic than average, in his white van) and rescue her from the doldrums of impending singledom. A fate worse than death!

She imagined that her Mr Right would do no wrong: he'd shower her with flowers; compliment her with the sweet stuff like "You needn't wear make-up, you're prettier without," and would generally be a suck-up without being a sap. He would be tall, dark AND handsome, and live up to her idealized image of the perfect man. His passion, devotion and loving feeling would know no bounds and her relationship would never grow stale. Admit it, that hopeless romantic was you!

In the quest for your perfect match you left no stone, pub or club unturned, leaving an army of dejected and rejected suitors and sweethearts in your wake: Mr Blue was too miserable and you didn't like that thing he did with his pinky; Mr Red got into too many scrapes after a few too many; and Mr Pink – well, looking back, perhaps his record-breaking collection of Kylie memorabilia should have been a clue? Or was it when you found his radio was tuned to Gaydar that you finally cottoned on?

But maybe such colourful characters weren't your thing and you were drawn magnetically to bad boys, getting off on getting chucked, and hanging out with bounders, boozers and losers? Yes, just what was it about the addiction to friction in a relationship when you were in your 20s? That tendency towards falling for those who'd sooner pick a fight than pick out a ring? Was it because deep down you knew you didn't want to meet the right guy yet? You were having too much fun!

"And do you, Timothy, though in the words of the bride 'not Mr. Right', promise as a poor second best to remain faithful and dutiful..."

In any case, there came a time when, likely as not, you realized enough was enough (and I mean enough after 100 wannabe wooers), and you had to follow the time-honoured tradition in matters of love – you settled for second best, and settled down too! And did you not, when the time came to do so, think, "Hmm, I'd like someone solid but not staid, someone jolly but not molly, someone fun but not fanatically so." Someone, perhaps… like your DAD?

And could this mean you may have to face the terrible truth, that even in terms of choosing a life partner you are, wait for it… turning into your Mum?

WHEN MR RIGHT BECOMES MR WRONG

For, as the march of time strides on, another sure-fire sign that you have the makings of your Mother is your attitude to men, in particular to the man in your life. When you were courting, things were different: you simply could not get enough of him, clinging to him like a limpet, hanging onto his every word and even to his trouser leg. You felt a sense of loss every time he went some place without you, even when he was just leaving the room. If he went on a boys' night out you lived in fear of him mingling with a bevy of man-crazed beauties, tempting him away from you with a flick of the eye.

Currently, as years of coupledom begin to take their toll, you relish the chance of a night off! Rare they are too, since his bum seems to be a permanent fixture in his favourite armchair in front of the telly. So, when a night of freedom from him hogging the remote control, inelegantly reminding you of what he had for dinner, and generally being a pest comes along you try not to show your ecstatic glee. And if he says he's off for a night out with the lads, you suggest innocently, "Why not make a weekend of it?" And, "I hear Timbuktu's nice this time of year!"

Then, it dawns on you why your own Mum was only too happy to iron Dad's shirt or polish his shoes if he was heading out of an evening – she couldn't wait to get rid of him! (And unlike in the days when you and she hoped your boyfriend, husband or live-in lover would be faithful, you live in the small hope that someone might be daft enough to start an affair with him!) Just like a carbon copy of her, once the front door is closed (with a bang of course – why can't men do anything quietly?), you stick *The Sopranos* on the telly, pour yourself a G & T and do your nails. Joy of joys!

And if he comes home early just as you're tucked up in bed with a bar of Galaxy and a good book (no doubt moaning about the price of a pint and how pubs just aren't the same anymore), you humph wearily "Men!" with the gusto that only your martyr of a mother could muster.

But let's not be too negative. There's every chance he'll be randy after several lager shandies, merry after a few sherries – you never know your luck. So, put aside that book, assume the position, and hope to hell he'll succumb to your charms and not to "brewer's droop". Lights out, Mum!

ABSENT-MINDEDNESS MAKES THE HEART GROW LESS FOND

His attitude to you also speaks volumes about the inevitable slippage into parental emulation. Wasn't it a bore when your Mum used to complain that Dad had lost his loving feeling? "Good," you selfishly thought in those days, nothing worse than seeing your parents getting all lovey-dovey as you try to munch on your cornflakes! Now you see her point, as little by little your own evenings of candle-lit meals and fine wine are on the decline. You can be sure you won't come across romantic love tokens left around the house, and compliments are usually of the back-handed kind – "Yes, that dress is lovely, it hides your bingo wings" – as he starts to Take You For Granted.

The days have also gone when he remembered significant dates: birthdays, anniversaries, and even – one year – Christmas! It's fairly certain you're becoming more like your Mum when you have to remind 'him indoors' of his own parents' birthdays... And you can be 100 per cent sure you're not at the first stop on the train to Mum-land, but have reached the final destination, when you have to buy their cards and presents too!

But the crowning glory of this abject asbent-mindedness, the thing you perhaps lament the most, is when the only floral tributes you receive are not on your anniversary, but when you've come indoors from doing the gardening and he says, "The roses are coming up nicely and what a fine petunia!" And said without a hint of irony, mind you.

"Let me guess, it's not a book, or a film...er,
it's our wedding anniversary."

At this point you'd be forgiven for saying, "Yes, and the
manure in the garden's as plentiful as the ***** that comes
out your mouth! How many more hints do you need: just
buy me a bouquet, you old fool!"

As his memory thusly deteriorates and his hairline
starts wearing thin, so does your patience, and the
things that you might have loved about him when you

first met begin to annoy the hell out of you. You might, for instance, have been attracted to his encyclopaedic knowledge, churning out facts and figures on a wide variety of subjects at every opportunity. These days, if you hear the words, "Now, didn't I read somewhere that..." one more time, you think you may make him swallow a dictionary – literally!

Oh come on. He can't be that bad, surely! Well, maybe... But I'll grant you one further irritation, that – even more so than you – he is becoming as socially adept as a dormouse, who'd do anything possible to hibernate his way through the party season! As such, and as he becomes more set in his ways, you have to dream up ingenious strategies to get him out the front door, such as: "No dear, of course it's not fancy dress, but you would look ever so sexy dressed as Batman/Shrek/Jon Bon Jovi" (take your pick according to your latest mid-life fantasy). Or, appealing to his mushrooming frugal mindset – "Don't worry, it's the Maynards' turn to pay." And if both those attempts fail there's always the tried and tested, "Yes, I will do that when we get home," counting on his falling fast asleep the minute his head hits the pillow!

FORGET BOYFRIENDS ARE THE NEW BLACK, GIRLFRIENDS ARE THE NEW BOYFRIENDS

And if you do go out together, say to a party, unlike in times when parties were about getting frisky and being frisky with the opposite sex, now you'd sooner stand at the opposite end of the room and moan about men instead! Indeed, as you become more like your Mum, you prefer your proximity to most men to be like ships that pass in the night – and stealth submarines at that. You're not taking any chances and will avoid men at most costs!

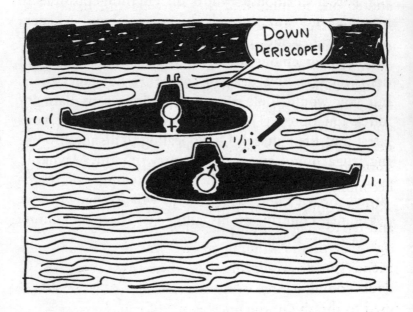

These new rules of un-attraction as middle age approaches mean you hang out more frequently with girl-friends, making up for the lost time spent in your twenties when you ditched them for aforementioned Mr Right.

Like in those heady days of youth, you can spend hours gossiping about men with your girly chums. But not quite in the same way. It would be boring as hell to re-peat the same conversations again and again – you know, "Does he fancy me?" "Do I fancy him?" "If he fancies me might I be able to force myself to fancy him?" And so on, and so on, ad infinitum, till you were an, ahem, item. And much, or indeed most, of your girly gossip may have revolved about how to get a particular fella into bed or down the aisle…

Right now, it's more than likely that much of your natter about nuptials will be how to get him out of it and out of your marriage! Yes, in matters of love, it's a rite of nearing-middle-age passage when the first of your friends starts to talk about splitting up as her Mr Right is fast becoming Mr Wrong!

So, as your forties or fifties cast their beady eye over you and try to drag you into their clutches, perhaps the first sign that they're winning is when the first among your friends gets divorced. And your Mum's own shadow is no doubt looming large over you when the kitchen table is used to thrash out the finer points of your friends' ailing love lives rather than to thrash out hours of lovemaking à la *Postman Always Rings Twice* as it might have done in years previous or rather in year previous (singular); i.e. the year that you met.

"Thongs for the memory."

Speaking of which, let's take a sneaky peek into the bedroom, which is perhaps where we'll find our most concrete evidence of all that, in matters of the opposite sex and love, you are becoming more and more like your mother. Calm down ladies! We're not talking about what's gathering dust in the bedside table! I'm talking of course about having a root around in your knickers drawer. For there's nothing that says Mum more than a multipack of briefs from Marks & Spencer. And a multipack of granny pants, mind you, as you've bid a sensible, knickered farewell to the thongs, midis and micro panties of your youth.

Of course if we delved a little further back in the drawer we might find something lacy and racy. It's not that sex isn't on the agenda at all any more! Men do still have certain uses...

Well, while we're in the bedroom and before we put the subject of men to bed, it would be remiss of me to omit any single women out there who are circling round middle age like vultures round a corpse (although perhaps with less enthusiasm). Don't think that being a spicy singleton helps you escape the evil clutches of the hand of middle age. Far from it! The single budding Mum has all the more opportunity to become set in her ways, stay home and generally become more straitlaced. Why not get out there and visit websites aimed just at you, the more "mature" woman, looking for lurve? How could you resist? Quite easily, I should imagine. Nobody to "helpfully" remark on your increasing middle-aged spread, nobody to fall asleep in front of the telly with, nobody to insist on another family camping holiday...

OH BOY! WHAT A LOOKER!

If this hasn't put you off, and you do still fancy bagging a bloke, or you just feel like a new one, don't worry! For, as you get older and less picky, the old saying "plenty more fish in the sea" comes into its own as a veritable shoal of fanciable older men presents itself to you.

You fancy them, don't you, those grey-haired men who you previously viewed as lost souls to help with a kindly arm across the road, or as possible candidates to play Santa Claus at your kids' Xmas party? Hell, yes! You've decided that silver foxes are, well, foxy and that the mature man has a suave air of sophistication that the younger generation lacks. Now, we're not talking George Clooney here; he's practically a baby compared to the characters you are starting to appreciate for the first time. We're thinking more along the lines of fancying Bill Clinton, so that when he earnestly delivers a speech on world poverty, he tugs at more than just your heart strings…

And older men do seem so much more attractive, you muse, when you see these young 'uns wearing their low-slung jeans sans underpants. Just what IS so sexy, you tut-tut in a school-marmish way, about revealing your bum crack? When you catch yourself thinking, "and surely he'll catch cold if he doesn't pull his trousers up?", you shudder with the realization that you're turning a corner into the one-way street of mumsiness.

And when you actually mutter out-loud, "Pull your trousers up, Son," there's no doubt you've taken that corner at full-pelt and are zooming down the long winding road to Mum-Land, faster than you'd care to.

"You misheard. I said young men bring out the
'smothering' instinct in me."

I know, I know, you're not past it yet, I'm sure you still give men in their twenties the glad eye. It's just that if they eye you curiously back, you come over all hot and flustered and pretend you had a twitch! Besides, estimating the age of good-looking lads becomes ever more difficult to judge – he could be a baby-faced and fanciable 30 or a mature-looking and Very Wrong 21. Better to be sensible and set your who's-hot and who's-not radar to those who appear to be well over 30.

Oh well, you'll just have to give up trying to pull them and do with this younger age group what Mums do best – mother them. Let's be honest – there's nothing you like more these days than making a cup of tea if the builders are in, especially if they're boyish and fresh-faced, and calling them "love" or "dear". And – let's be fair as well as honest – there would be no harm in engineering yourself an opportunity to squeeze past them in a doorway or on the stairs. Such is your maternal aura, they wouldn't suspect a thing!

HIM TARZAN, YOU JANE

You're so good at busying yourself, making cups of tea and getting into your new role as charwoman and general flunky, aren't you?

Of course, it wasn't always so! There was a time when you were quite the independent woman, weren't you? You single-handedly removed terrifying spiders from the bath, changed plugs and knew where the fusebox was.

If you had to take your car in for a service you boned up beforehand so you wouldn't be ripped off. You were a dab hand at DIY, and knew one end of a power drill from the other.

However, as you slip into middle age and your comfy slippers, so you are probably slipping more comfortably into traditional male/female roles than you did in your youth. Take driving for instance. In your youth you were known as something of a speed freak, zooming around town on your moped, or tearing it up down country lanes in your 2CV or Mini Cooper. Now, if a family drive is the order of the day, you reluctantly take out the map as your husband dons his leather driving gloves with a deeply contented sigh. Well, anything to keep the grumpy old git happy!

You've handed over responsibility for much of the "manly" stuff indoors too. That's possibly down to the simple fact that it makes him feel, well, manly, for doing it. Thusly you devolve the tasks of opening jars/putting up shelves/doing mucky plumbing jobs to the man in your life. Even if you know you could do it as well – or better. Well, sometimes it pays to play up your feminine side and you know there's nothing he likes more than to feel useful!

It's not that you've become more girly. Far from it. It's just that you've learnt that a little bit of give and take goes a long way in the battle of the sexes, that with age comes wisdom, and it's a wise woman who knows when to play up her feminine side to get what she wants from her fella.

When you start to think like this, when you don't even make an effort to change a light bulb, you may as well forget that you were once a feminist and give in with lady-like good grace to the ideals of your grand parents' generation!

Alright, alright! Perhaps you're not quite ready to lose your feminist credentials just yet. Not quite prepared to renounce 50 years of women's liberation in order to avoid dealing with that nasty blockage in the U-bend. Nonetheless you're increasingly realistic about the differences between the goose and the gander and have decided what's good for one isn't necessarily good for the other. Quite right too! Who wants to spend their life up a ladder, or down the loo. Not exactly ladylike is it?

Chapter 4

Retail Therapy

In the mythology of our national press, it's often cited that, when surveyed, many women say they prefer shopping to sex. There's probably a good explanation for this. Such is stress of twenty-first-century living, such is the shortness of the modern attention span, the women possibly only answered "shopping" as it was the last thing they were doing before they were asked: I mean, it's likely such surveys are carried out in shopping malls, rather than in the privacy of your own bedroom...

"I'm sorry Guy.... I'm leaving you for John Lewis."

But you can understand why such comparisons are made. Let's think about the similarity between the two. The rise of the heart-rate as you swoop down on the object of your desire, the climactic thrill as the till rings out the cost of your purchase, and the post-climactic glumness when you get home and realize that the shop's mirror told you a pack of lies to win you over.

Still, this doesn't deter the young and the young at heart from doing the retail rounds at every opportunity. Any slip of a thing worth her salt will know what it is to "shop till you drop". Forget about binge-drinking, binge-shopping is her *raison d'être*, and she's not content unless she has wolfed down enormous quantities of consumerism, polished off by spending lashings of lolly on a weekly or even daily basis.

Prepare yourself, for, as you turn into your Mum, your whole shopping experience is set to change radically. Previously shopaholic females feel like they need a dose of actual therapy after the retail variety. No longer will you have time for shops where you can't tell the assistant from the shop dummies, who smirk when you ask for anything larger than a size zero, and who seem desperate to steer you off the premises before you frighten away the youngsters. As for the "high street" chains, as you slip into middle age it's more than likely you'll have the hideous realization that you're as out of place in Top Shop as a super model is at an "all-you-can-eat" buffet.

But, come on, really, do you want to shop there any more anyway? What with the ear-splitting music, the surly shop assistants and furnace-hot changing rooms, you might well be heard sighing, "Top Shop? Bottom shop, more like!" And let's be honest, it's not as if you even like, let alone *understand*, the clothes in there these days. But if you should, by some stroke of inordinate luck find a garment that's not too long (just in passing, why are clothes these days made for giraffes?), too tight, or too bizarre-looking, you're soon put off from ever shopping there again. The minute you hit the communal changing rooms and spy the sweaty swathes of nubile young bodies brazenly on display, you harrumph, "That's it. I'm off!"

SHUTTING UP SHOP(PING)

Whatever shall you do? It's not like Marx has won you over just yet – you do still need to buy stuff! Well, the answer is that, weirdly, as you follow in your Mum's footsteps – literally pacing behind her to find out where the fledgling Mum can get away with shopping – you fluctuate between two wildly opposing choices.

Firstly, the Mum-in-waiting is often seen to be frequenting the local boutique which usually has a name like "Cybil's" (Ooh, with that racy C rather than the standard English S, the shop must be "funky", you tell yourself. Well, if you insist…) In said boutique the assistant knows your name and your dress size, so you don't have to reveal too much on each visit. The clothes on display go up to an XXL – even if you don't need that size, it's ever so reassuring to know it's there. (Like Botox or Liposuction: good to know they exist, won't necessarily ever use them.)

"What about trying this on for size."

But sometimes you can't face the over-familiarity of Cybil's (and you feel somewhat conned when you spy some paperwork and discover she really is a Sybil), and you head for the anonymity of the indoor shopping mall. What is it about becoming a Mum which means you can spend so much time in such places, without developing a blinding headache like the rest of the population? Indeed if you were a superheroine it's likely your superpower would be your feet's remarkable resilience to pounding the mall floor for 10 hours. Then, there comes a time when you can't even face either of these options – so where does this leave you?

Fear not ladies. There's a secret every Mum up and down the land knows, a secret that is passed on from mother to daughter, spoken in hushed, reverential tones, when they feel their daughter has come "of age". When it all becomes too much, when you've not given up on a love of acquiring new things, but you can't bear the actual act of acquiring them, your Mum will pass on this knowledge. Come on, you have to promise not to tell if I reveal all here. Okay? Here goes. When all else fails, when the game is up on your pretence that you actually like shopping, you can always get what you need in *John Lewis*.

Aaah! Across the country, we hear a collective sigh of relief as the secret of your future happy retail consumption is let out of the (shopping) bag. Can you resist the values of a store where you know you will be "Never knowingly undersold?" Can you say no to the polite assistants when they offer you a store card? Can you afford NOT to spend all day in store including a visit to the fifth-floor café for lunch? Course you can't. And of course this means but one thing. Your new approach to shopping is the spine-chilling nadir of your transformation into your Mum.

SHOPPING "EXPEDITIONS"

In your youth you were far more adventurous in the shopping terrain you covered. The preferred landscape for your shopping sprees in "buy"-gone days were the mountainous peaks of the bargain bin or fighting your way through a chaotic forest of overloaded clothes rails, while your natural habitat was the concrete jungle of the local city or town centre. Your natural behaviour, and that of your consumer-crazy companions, was to travel in a pack.

For it is the, um, custom of the young female shopper to always hit the shops in groups. Look, there they go, and watch out anyone who stands in the way of their fashion frenzy! The leader of the pack, the alpha female shopper, preys ominously out front, always the one to haggle with the shopkeeper, or to waltz into a fancy-schmancy boutique in defiance of the watchful eyes of the store assistant, who defends her goods like a mother protecting her young! The rest of the pack skulk behind, eyes roaming here there and everywhere, always on the lookout for the last size 10 of the season's must-have item. (Must-have, that is, until the alpha shopper, dominant arbiter of taste and style, decrees said item soooo last year!)

Not any more. Now you fancy group shopping as much as you fancy group sex and size 10 is a figure (both meanings) that is probably a dim and distant memory! As for trying to convince your husband or partner to join you for a spot of retail therapy, forget about it! You're too long in the tooth to think your menfolk will accompany you. They'd rather have a tooth pulled!

So, now, armed only with a plethora of environmentally-friendly cotton shoppers, you prefer to shop alone. Well, you only need cover the five floors of John Lewis and the food hall in M & S – you can be in and out of town in no time!

Mind you, I say, *prefer* to go shopping alone but the chances are there is one small accoutrement which sadly you can't do without. Not so much a fashion accessory as a biological necessity. Yep, it's those blasted kiddiewinks again. Granted, when they're babies, they're no bother – there's no end to the charm of the little people, and shop assistants like nothing more than to bounce a newborn or infant around on their knee. Oh dear, little Terry has puked over that two hundred quid silk dress. Never mind, the shop assistant coos. Indeed the only worry you might have when out shopping with the baby, so little trouble are they, is that you might leave them in their buggy in the home furnishings department.

No such luck with anything that can walk. It's as if the minute your little darling reaches his first birthday, shop assistants are automatically set to "worry mode". Sure, it was OK for baby to puke all over that designer frock, but toddlers can't cut any such slack when they manhandle

Habitat's best china or get sticky paws all over their linens. Nor is it possible to simply whip out your breast or a dummy to pacify little Terry when he's screaming, "I want a cookie," or "I've done a pooooooo!" So, when the store detectives come to scrape the kicking and screaming body off the floor, you realize that the game is up on shopping being any fun. Especially when the kicking, screaming body is not your toddler's but your own...

FEMAIL ORDER

No wonder you take a leaf out of your Mum's book and develop a fervent love for the mail-order catalogue. And not any of the "cool" ones either. Rather, you cast an approving eye over the latest Hawkshead and Boden offerings. Worse yet, you naively think that some of the clothes in them are fashionable. So much nicer to shop from the comfort of your own armchair! So much more agreeable to try on clothes in the privacy of your own bedroom! So much... like your Mum!

But your increasing fondness for remote retail does not stop there. Oh no! Why, there is a whole world of online, mail-order and telephone shopping to discover. As such, you become postman's enemy number one as your daily dose of retail therapy lands – or rather thuds – on the doormat. Not that the entire postal service hates you: the fat cat bosses rather appreciate your business. For more often than not, you return your goodies from whence they came. Bloody misleading catalogue photos!

"Mummy... one of my friends says you can watch films
and cartoons and stories on TV as well."

And let's not get started on the TV shopping channels. Come on, admit it. In spite of yourself, you've been sucked in by the chummy chatting of her on QVC, you can't help but believe her promise that the floaty gypsy skirt in 12, count 'em, 12 gorgeous sultry shades will be sold out in 10, 9, 8… Quick, grab the phone and get one. Better yet, get two: one for you and one for you know who!

Rather pleased with yourself, aren't you? You've found a way to shop until you drop without the inconvenience of err, shopping, or dropping! However, your new hobby probably won't last long – as soon as the bank statement comes through the door and you see the number of late night Saturday purchases, the result of drunken directory dialling, your common sense and stinginess get the better of you. Until next time, that is.

SUPERMARKET SWEEP

There are many mini-tragedies that could befall your family – you could lose your job, your just-turned-teenage daughter could come home with a bloke twice her age and half her charm and intelligence, the dog could get diarrhoea and spray it over your new cashmere throw (white of course). But none of these compare to the following worst-case scenario, the Mother (ahem) of all indications that your maternal mutation has begun.

This is when, on using the lav, only a scrap of loo paper dangles off the roll, or while washing your hands, the soap has worn down to a minuscule morsel, or when, on putting on a brew, one solitary coffee granule stares back at you from the jar… and there is no replacement to be found in the cupboard! Shock! Horror! Dial 999. Better still, call your Mum! For it is only she who could possibly spare any sympathy for this mountain you're making of that domestic molehill.

"We've customized our own bendy trolley to cut down on supermarket visits."

Just like her, in order to avoid the calamity of running out of anything in future you now plan your food shopping with military precision. Yes, even your approach to the weekly shop is changing as you wave a white flag to oncoming middle age. In the past it was so easy to pick up something after work, dash into the local supermarket and knock up some pasta and pesto or an oven-ready meal. If you ran out of loo roll, you stole some from work or used your flatmate's expensive facial cleansing wipes. Basically, if you ran out of basics you didn't run out of the house at 90 miles an hour, waving your arms with comic exaggeration to stop the local shopkeeper turning his sign to "Closed".

No chance of that now. Because you have come to know and love the value pack. Your maxim is now "bigger is better" as week after week you stuff your shopping trolley with bumper packs of cereal, 16 loo rolls, and all the tea in China. And if something's not good value, well it's quite simply no good.

Woe betide you if you don't buy in bulk, otherwise you may have to do something that any reasonable, right-thinking person will avoid at all costs, something you feel you've done more than you've had hot dinners, an excursion that brings you in the chilliest of cold sweats – the extra-curricular supermarket excursion. You know the one – the one you have to do on a Friday after work when the world and his wife are doing their weekly shop, and you just want a pint of milk, a loaf of bread and a two-litre bottle of vodka (which you've finished by the time it's your turn at the checkout).

HAPPY SHOPPER?

Well, well, not quite the happy shopper you used to be, are you? There's no finer indication of this than when the already dreaded shopping experience goes from bad to worse, when you've lugged your loot on a crowded, smelly bus, and you get home to discover that you have a faulty item.

"Let me through... I'm a retail therapist."

Uh-oh! Nothing gets you bent out of shape more than if your merchandize doesn't live up to your exacting standards, for as your number in years rises, so do your expectations. And boy, do you soon let everybody know about them.

Come on, get it off your chest. "They just don't make things like they used to, do they?" I mean, when you were a girl your family had the same telly for 30 years... in fact, isn't your Mum still watching the same one? Nowadays shoddy electrical goods come as standard and that's before we've even got started on clothing. Buttons not sewn on properly, hemlines glued instead of sewn, and everything's so bloody tight. Hmm, not sure you could get away with bringing the clothing company to book over that last one...

Anyway, you've got to pity the poor sales assistant who has to deal with your complaints. So accomplished have you become in venting your spleen that you bypass him or her immediately with your three-step plan for retail revenge. Step one: march confidently up to the counter and ask to speak to the manager. Don't take no for an answer. Step two: if your complaint isn't dealt with promptly enough or to your monetary satisfaction, get the bit between your teeth and move on to the area manager. Step three: still got a beef? Bombard the head office with phone calls and letters until they refund you that five quid... Gosh, that was worth the effort, wasn't it?

It's a wonder that you shop at all any more! And it's not just where and how you shop that's changed, but also when. No longer do you pound the pavement of a Saturday afternoon while your other half is at the footie, and just the words, "late-night shopping" are enough to bring you out in a rash. None of that out-of-hours activity for you! Instead you get up early to "beat the rush", happy in the company of the OAPs on the look-out for the supermarket's bargains of the day. Happy, let's not beat around the bush, in the company of all the other Mums!

You can spot them a mile off: far-off-rather-be-any-where-than-here look in the eye; determined gait as they march as if pre-programmed towards John Lewis; unwilling stroppy toddler, tweenie or teen in tow. Look, there goes one now! Grumpy of demeanour, wearing the requisite Mum jeans-boots-white T-shirt combo. Recognize her? Sure you do. It's you. Quick, get thee round the mall before everyone else gets out of bed!

Chapter 5

A Grey Area

Have you looked in the mirror recently? Of course you have. No self-respecting woman could pass any mirror without having a sneaky peek. Still, not quite the same experience as it used to be, is it? A few years ago, when you did so, you were likely to have been excessively self-critical – if you'd screwed your eyes up tight enough you might have spied a fine line here, a dark bag there. But a spot of concealer and a layer of foundation sorted out those minor wrinkles and cosmetic rankles, and you were soon happy enough with your appearance.

Now, looking into the mirror breeds more doom and gloom than looking into the dark depths of your very soul. You can't pass off the crevices criss-crossing your forehead or around your eyes as "laughter lines" anymore. In fact if anyone presumed to call these far-from-funny lines just that, you might well sock them one!

And, as the looking glass sneers unkindly back at you, you think, "I recognize that face…" but weirdly not as your own. Now, who does that venerable visage remind me of, you ponder? Nigella? No. You may be unleashing your inner Domestic Goddess in the kitchen, but sadly this is not reflected (both senses) when you look in the mirror. The late Princess Di? Hmm. Well, you've got the matching sensible hairdo but perhaps not the strong cheekbones and jawline. How about the hip woman's middle-aged style icon – Madonna? Fat chance. Maradona, more like.

It's someone else I resemble, you muse, someone a bit closer to home – who is it now, you continue, it's on the tip of my tongue? Then, as you open up the front door to that certain someone, you stand slack-jawed as you realize just whose mirror image you've become. We're talking, of course, about your Mum!

We've looked in other chapters at those little habits, the annoying mannerisms and bad manners, the clichéd sayings, you might have picked up from her. But perhaps the deadliest, most annoying sign that you're turning into your Mum is when people stop you in the street and mistake you for her!

OVER MY DEAD BODY

How did you let this happen? As a young woman, you'd have done anything not to look like her. If you had the same hair colour you dyed yours pink to avoid maternal emulation, and if you shared the same-shaped hooter, you might have contemplated plastic surgery. Even if this meant making a perfectly straight nose wonky! If someone had told you that one day you would look like her, you'd have mumbled, "Over my dead body." In fact you thought that was about as likely as that you would ever die – you were going to live forever!

In those halcyon days before you gave anything too much thought, even if you had a similar look to your Mum, it's likely you would have only borne a passing resemblance to her... the odd twinkle in your eye here, the odd gesture there. And when it came to "weighty" matters, while you were busy scoffing all the pies, she was watching the scales with an eagle-eye. Come on, admit it, you would sometimes giggle tactlessly at her worrywart – or rather worry-weight – phrases about her increasing girth, like the timeless "Once on the lips, forever on the hips." How times change! Now you're loathe to admit she was right, and these words have become your mantra as your metabolism slows down – and your weight gain speeds up!

Not that it's entirely your Mother's fault that you're metamorphosing into her. (Snide comments and years of grinding you down about your personal taste and style aside…) No, it's another Mother we have to blame for your gradual transformation into your Mum's personal Looky-Likey. The Mother of all Mothers, the bee-atch who decrees it inevitable that – as the relentless slip into your middle years approaches – you will turn into your Mother. And that's Mother Nature.

Just what is it about her? She counts rainbows, waterfalls and other delightful natural wonders among her brethren. But there's no doubt she was having an off day when she decided to work on the scientific certitude that you will some day turn into your Mum: genes and heredity. The result of this genetic handywork being that, as you mature, as the march of time goes on, your body will shape-shift into that of your Mum is. And with it being a genetic inheritance, you've as much chance of escaping it as you do your eye colour or shoe size. Bloody science!

"I think if we're both honest, Deirdre, we'd have to agree that your days here as a lapdancer are numbered."

Pity really, as among those things we've picked up from your own Mum and from the big Mother N are the following little foibles: what once went up must now – thanks to gravity, kids and those pesky genes again – come down (of course we're talking about boobs). Your previously crease-free face now looks like a crinkle-cut crisp. Last, but not least, the spare tyre around your waist shows no sign of deflating – no matter how much air you let out!

The problem is, as your body demands you do an increasing amount of frenetic aerobic activity to get rid of these lumps and bumps, so you desire a workout of a more sedate nature. Indeed, you can't think of anything worse than bopping around in a stuffy gym, listening to repetitive beats, watching your flabby bits bouncing up and down in the mirror next to a well-toned youngster who seems to have no boobs at all.

But if you can't quite give up the notion of paying to contort your body into unnatural poses, you take up a gentler form of exercise such as pilates or yoga instead of aerobics or step. In the golden-olden days trying out new positions was something you did – well, you know what for. Nowadays, the only new positions you dare try out are on the yoga mat, as you limber up for your starring role as your Mum's body double!

Well, well, that's quite some effort you're putting into your appearance there. And there's nothing that says this more than the amount of time and money you now spend in the beauty salon. Don't deny it! Barings Bank execs would even choke when they see how much you're robbing your own bank to shell out on beauty treatments.

Let's think for a moment here about your beauty routine as a young lassie. Hair-washing was a weekly task (or more frequent if you needed an excuse to say no to the swathes of boys inviting you out on a date). You might have purchased the odd mud mask from Boots for 99p if you were off on a night out and you made do with this same shop's own-brand cleansing and moisturizing products.

You can't get away with things that easily these days! Now you deem it necessary to spend as much as your number of years on anti-ageing products – the one area of your life where you believe luxury is a necessity. In fact, your penchant for pampering is so compulsive that they should invent a new term to describe you – a pamperholic! The pamperholic is a frighteningly elegant beast, frequenting the beauty salon more often than your old man hits the pub. Yes, you may have mocked your own Mother for her constant preening, primping, fussing and flossing. But, as you change into her, so you have to hold your well-mani-cured hands up to being a pamperholic yourself!

If beauty salons herald a new dawn for you as "Mum", then spending time at a health farm must usher in the whole darn dawn chorus. Now, us humans, we're suppos-edly the most intelligent beings on Earth. Call this a gift from God, call it the wonder of science, call it what you will. But I'm pretty sure whoever put us here didn't intend for grown women to take so much pleasure from donning a luxury towelling dressing-gown, starving themselves for a week, and then shaking all their wobbly bits with similarly mummified women in an aqua-aerobics class!

As if this wasn't enough, you decide that you need to reach out to your inner beauty and take up an unhealthy interest in mediums, tarot cards and crystals. Your mantra becomes "a healthy mind in a healthy body". No prizes for guessing where you picked up this little gem of a phrase. I don't think you need me to tell you that when such new-age nonsense appears there's only a ghost of chance that you can – mind, body AND spirit – avoid the mutation into your Mum.

A GREY AREA

But perhaps the crowning glory, the topmost, the *head* reason that your looks are headed in one inevitable direction, is one particular aspect of your appearance. Hmm. Can you guess from the rather obvious hints here? Yes, we're talking, of course, about your hair. There's nothing like that first one on your chinny-chin-chin, or the first grey strand on your head, to make you feel that you're embarking on a new journey in life, and there's no surer sign that you've reached your destination than when you find a wiry grey one south of the border...

Although it would be remiss of me to suggest that going grey around the gusset is the most hair-raising (geddit!) thing that can happen to your once lustrous locks, your once beautiful and bountiful barnet. I mean, it's not like anyone apart from your beautician and lover will notice. No sirree, it's when the hairs on your head lose their sultry smoothness, frizz up and start to resemble pubes... then you've really got to worry.

"I'm devastated... I found a long grey hair on his suit this morning. Instead of lying and telling me he had another woman, the bastard points out that it's one of mine!"

Bloody hell. Down to the hairdressers sharpish! Not that you decide to compensate for this hideous hirsuteness with a funky, modern hairdo. Far from it. Gone are the days when you waltzed into the hairdressers with an image torn from a magazine of a 1980s poodle perm or asked for the ubiquitous '90s, 'Rachel'. As for the unflattering asymmetrical styles sported by the yoof of today, you'd rather shave it all off or wear a silly wig than be seen dead with one of them!

Nope, you've learned the lesson from nightmarish, ugly hairdos gone by that your hair won't do as it's told. Better to opt instead for a nice sensible bob, or Princess Di crop. So much more manageable like that, wouldn't your dear Mama have said? And manageable is what you need for tresses that once were lustrous and pliable, but can now only be tamed by a gallon of de-frizzing lotion – and that's just what's needed before you'll even get out of bed in the morning!

As for those grey hairs, well, you know you are en route to imitation-central when dying your hair isn't just an experiment to see how you'd look as a blonde, but an absolute necessity. And you know you could be crowned queen of the Mum copycats when you feel it necessary to lie about it: "Why, yes, rich, deep chocolate or sweet as honey blonde is my natural colour, thanks for asking," you say with a steely look that nobody would ever dare to question!

As for "down-below," well, up to you if you prefer dying to lying. Just remember the golden rule: drapes and rug should match.

THE HEIGHT OF FASHION

You're nearly all set for your mumsy make-over, but let's not forget one very important factor you'll need to make your transformation complete, and that's your clothing. There is nothing like the costume drama that is choosing clothes to make you feel like your time has come to be like your Mum.

Even basic things, like getting dressed of a morning, make you feel that the euphemistic "prime of life" is on its way. Back in the day you shamelessly slid naked out of bed – possibly not your own – and into a hastily thrown-together outfit, and your motto might have been "less is more". Simply adding a brooch or dangly earrings lent an air of fizz and sparkle to your outfit. You didn't have to try hard to look cool and getting dressed was as easy as making a cup of tea – and took about the same amount of time.

As you take more and more after your Mum, you don't slide or bounce out of bed, but cautiously reveal one toe at a time, and shyly keep the rest covered up until your partner has left the room. Only then will you head for your wardrobe for an item that respects your modesty as much as your duvet does! And it's a walk-in wardrobe of course, since your advancement in years means you have acquired a whole range of ill-fitting and ill-advisedly purchased clothing. Well, you never know when it will come back into style, and you know, "waste not, want not!"

Pah! You're crazy! Yukky 1970s flares; bulbous '80s puff-balls; "Frankie says Relax" T-shirts; too-tight black leggings – they'll never come back into style. Whoops! My bad. But being right only makes you more mumsy, so neh!

"I know I complimented you on that outfit last
time you wore it, but that was 1980."

Anyway style isn't really what floats your boat any more is it? Nope, comfy clothing is where it's at these days, sister! Yes, it's clear you are rolling up your sleeves, ready to play the part of your Mum when your clothing becomes functional not funky, and it's fairly certain that the curtain has come down on your previous life for good when your outfit has more layers than a Viennetta.

It should come as no surprise, then, that your favouritest of all wardrobe favourites should be the cardigan, that most versatile, comfy and stylish of items, which – more importantly – can be whipped on and whipped off quicker than you can say, "hot flush!" Ah, the cardigan! You can dress it up, you can dress it down, you can wear it in, but whatever you do, if you're becoming like your Mum, make sure you wear it out... By which I mean put it on so often that the elbows have worn thinner than your ever-decreasing patience for "high fashion". I'm nobody's fool though, I'm well aware that you don't own just one cardigan! Bloomin' Nora, no! An entire cotton field has been picked of its buds in order to equip you with a cardy in every style, length and colour imaginable.

Having established that you're becoming a fully paid-up member of club cardigan, let's continue southwards down the body, for further evidence of your wardrobe's decline into middle-agedom: your choice of footwear. Your shoes used to be the, ahem, height of fashion as you tottered about in five-inch heels (that were one-tenth of an inch across the base – the more the heel looked like a lethal weapon, the better). Now, you follow in your Mum's (sensibly heeled) footsteps and while selecting a new pair of, say, sandals or boots, you mutter grumpily to the shop assistant, "Well, they're all right of course, but do you have anything in a lower heel… or in brown? ('And my goodness, should she be allowed to work here – isn't she like 12?)"

"But hold on," you protest, "I've just as many pairs as I had in my youth. Doesn't that count for something?" Well, yes, but instead of countless shoes that were good for dancing and romancing, you now own 20 pairs of comfy walking, hiking and biking boots!

Tut-tut, you're quite the un-snappy dresser these days aren't you? And not without good reason. Why would you go hell for – well, leather, or don a mini-skirt or thigh-high boots when that sartorial slur that maturing women everywhere have come to know and dread may cruelly pass someone's lips: "She's mutton dressed as lamb!" So, you set what's come to be known as your "mutton monitor" to high, and avoid wearing anything too revealing, too tight or too fancy – well, not at the same time, anyway.

As for clothes that were "cool" in your twenties and early thirties, such as cargo pants, biker boots and trainers, put these on at your peril as they're no longer deemed fashionable and you may just be showing your age if you dare to wear!

Don't think this means that you're any less likely to be judged as "mutton" if you wear contemporary fashions – no matter how good you might think you look in them. Not that it's likely you'd fancy giving noughties styles a whirl – for goodness' sake, you didn't like high-waisted jeans or puffball skirts the first time they were in fashion!

No wonder that you are coming around to the idea of settling for muted shades and longer lengths – that you think it best to try and blend into the background – when the fashion police seem so keen to knock at your door. This is especially true if you have teenagers around who'd do anything for you not to look "different". Hence, your "trendy threads" no longer see the light of day. Whoops. Even when *talking* about fashion, you are starting to imitate your Mum!

Luckily there is a time when you do go to (tinsel) town with your clobber, when you throw caution – and mutton – to the wind, and your love of sparkly clothes and accessories comes into its own. And that is, of course, Christmas. Come on, 'fess up, as soon as you began to feel slightly over the hill, there was nothing you liked more than to over-compensate by wearing comedy dangly earrings that could be mistaken for Christmas baubles and a glittery blouse or jumper that has "Help! I'm turning into my Mum" written all over it. Not literally, of course. Yet.

Well, the wardrobe mistress has been in, you've been into hair and make-up and you're now ready to blow a lipsticked kiss of death to the carefree days of youth and play your new starring role as your Mum. Not that you can spend too much time enjoying the fruits of your labour. It took you twice as long to look half as good as you used to and the cab has been waiting for half an hour. Hurry along, Mum!

Not so fast though! Just when you'd convinced yourself you could dare to bare in a particularly revealing outfit, in walks your teenage daughter. Is she teasing as she says, matter-of-factly, "I didn't know it was fancy dress. Austrian barmaid is it?" Then, just as you ready yourself, dreaming up a killer comeback, your teenage son follows your first born, and says, less discreetly, 'Christ, Mum, put it away!" Well, at least they didn't accuse you of looking like their gran. Thank heavens for small mercies!

Chapter 6

Girls Just Don't Want To Have Fun

There was a time in your life when you were quite the party girl, wasn't there? Out with your chums until all hours, raising merry hell as you gadded gaily about, you were the personification of fun itself. As time goes by, though, you've swapped the pub for a trug; parties for weeding, breeding and reading as gardening, babies and books have begun to swallow your social life whole. In fact, your calendar – marked with an abundance of quiet nights in, and conspicuously lacking any wild nights out – seems to be turning into a carbon copy of someone else's. (Yup, it's her again!)

If you do receive an invitation to a party, your reaction is a telltale sign that you're becoming ever more like her. Instead of whooping with delight and stocking up on party poppers, you're fast becoming a party-pooper, armed with a wide and imaginative array of excuses why it's impossible for you to attend. Indeed, you'd rather be laid up with a cold than risk being laid out flat after a night of excess.

Hence, "the baby-sitter/children/other half's sick," or, "my piles are playing up," trip off your tongue as easily as, "the dog ate it," did when you'd forgotten to do your homework. Come to think of it, your attendance at school was better than your current efforts at showing your face at parties. And that's saying something.

"Just hold out upstairs Geraldine...
they're doing the Conga now !"

I COULD HAVE DANCED ALL NIGHT ... BUT MY FEET WERE KILLING ME

Equally telling is your behaviour if you run out of said excuses and do grace the host with your presence. On arrival you scan the room for a comfy chair farthest from the speakers. "And what *is* that noise they're blasting out," you mutter to yourself? Surely the DJ should stick on some *Blondie* or *Happy Mondays* to get the dance floor going?"

A wee while ago you might have been the one to get the party started, mumbling, "I'll show these young 'uns how it's done," but now you honestly can't remember how! (And let's face it, you're a bit out of breath after walking up three flights of stairs to the top flat.) So there you sit, tapping your foot to a song you don't know, or like, smiling wanly at the guests as they start to dance by.

Your alcohol consumption is no less lame, as you avoid the spirits and rum punch, sensibly drinking a glass of water for each glass of wine; and, instead of counting up the number of drinks you've imbibed to brag to your mates later, you're counting down the minutes until you can leave. And so, as soon as a respectable amount of time has passed, you slip away discreetly. You needn't worry, though. It's not like anybody noticed you were there in the first place... So off you can trot on your merry – but definitely not drunken – way!

Of course these days it's far more likely that any invitation that pops through the letterbox is for one of your teenage kids, whose social lives are more active than yours by a long chalk. When it arrives, you breathe a sigh of relief that the invite isn't for you, only to remember that it's your turn to do the chauffeuring. "What am I?" you bellow, your own Mum's words coming back to haunt you. "A blooming taxi service?"

And if your kids are still so young that you have to stay for the proceedings, you hope to God the parents will serve alcohol. Unlike at the adult parties you attend, you drink to excess at kiddy dos to cope with the inevitable sugar-fuelled strops and repetitious conversations with the other parents. Typically these start with a minor embarrassment ("Sarah, isn't it?" "Natalie, actually") and continue inexorably to formulaic comparisons of your child's academic career to Natalie, Actually's daughter. You soon realize that Natalie, Actually has no other topic than how great her child is, and when she utters "She really was the best sheep in the nativity play," you have no option but to head off for yet another glass of wine.

Your dislike of parties (for big and little people) soon helps you come to terms with the fact that you prefer the comfort of your own four walls of an evening. As soon as you've had this epiphany, the death knell is duly sounded for the girls' night out. Not that you've stopped socializing altogether, you've simply decreed "staying in is the new going out," spending much more time at home or at your friends' houses than you do in pubs or clubs. As you usher in this new dawn of domesticity and decorum, the hand of fate is surely waving you on to new levels of sensibleness, and when your girls' nights start to involve some form of cultural or practical activity, you realize to your horror that you've reached the point of no return!

BLUESTOCKING, *MOI*!

A popular choice for the girls' night in is the book group, which, strangely enough, somehow makes reading much less fun. Before it was an occasional pleasure and you might have had your nose in a book every now and then – perhaps a spot of non-fiction, such as *How To Look Thin While Eating Cake* or the latest whodunnit, chick-lit romance or equally light-weight tome. Then, in a bid to get out (or more accurately in) more, increase your IQ and generally be more arty-farty-girl than party-girl, you joined or found a reading group.

Here, you ostensibly get together with your girlfriends to have a little drink and convivial chat about a book, but the atmosphere soon turns more competitive than a Mums' race at school sports day, more heated than the burning pits of Hades, and boozier than at a piss-up in the proverbial. All because nobody can agree which book to read that month. Various techniques can be used to make this decision easier: you can try going around the group alphabetically, or by people's birthdays, or which of you bangs the table the loudest and looks like she might cry. Conversely, perhaps you punish whoever left the book unfinished last time, by not letting her have a turn. Oh, whoops. That'd be all of you… Best stick to plan A!

Plan A being preferable to admitting that while the idea of a book group appeals, the reality of chewing the fat about a book you haven't read is more tedious than sitting through Mr French's English class at school. (You remember the one. The teacher who couldn't be bothered to actually teach so dictated lines from his favourite poetry books. And depressing Siegfried Sassoon poems at that.) Anyway, I digress.

"I see you've dressed to go clubbing !"

If it's your turn to choose, thank heavens, as you're sick of reading other people's uninspired and ill-informed choices. Don't blow your chance! You'll want to come across as well-read but not show-offy, intelligent but not intimidating, to gain kudos with the girls. So, when it's your turn why not suggest a title that you've read before and save yourself the worry of suggesting a turkey? (And having to read the blinking thing in the first place.)

A key feature of the reading group, as suggested, is that often most of you haven't made it past chapter three or even the introduction. It's therefore a good place to practice the art of bluffing and keeping a poker face. If you're feeling panicked about not having made it to the end, you can always rent the DVD film version the night before. Let's be honest and all hold our hands up to that one! But of course you checked beforehand that the book had the same ending as the film... Didn't you?

Perhaps you've already taken all of the above into account, and the reading group does not appeal, so you joined a stitch and bitch club, or sewing circle, instead. Yes, you used to swear that knitting and making your own clothes was embarrassing when your Mum did it, especially when she made you not only admire, but model, her handi-work. These days you're counting the pennies, though, and isn't the home-made touch so much nicer? Granny certainly thinks so when you take the kids round to hers in their matching Fair Isle sweaters!

Oh dear! You're becoming quite the homebody aren't you, what with your stitching and bitching, quiet nights in, and life without sin? The winds of change are certainly blowing away the propensity you had for all-nighters or even a simple late night. Quite right too! Party-hardy makes you tardy and we couldn't have that, could we Mum? Why, it's a waste of a day to malinger in bed until noon, especially when you have to get into town or to work early in order to beat the rush.

THE HOSTESS WITH THE MOSTEST

Not that you *never* throw your own parties, just that they are now much more civilized affairs. Unlike those of your youth, where being a "host" took on a biological meaning – that is, your home was simply the empty shell where partying parasites would come to suck the lifeblood out of good taste and good behaviour, kicking up their heels – and throwing up their drinks – and quite simply you would not care. Next week you'd be at their place, doing the very same. Youthful spontaneity and *laissez-faire*-ness meant party planning involved a quick trip to the mini-mart a few hours before to stock up on lagers, mixers, a few bags of nuts and – if you had your thinking cap on – bin bags to clear up the debris the next day.

As you make a break from this hedonistic hell-raising of the past, as mentioned, parties are becoming much more tame. Yes, you still like to hold the odd do – indeed you are the venerable Hostess With The Mostest – but these days your soirées are planned with almost military precision. Not least if you surrender to that epicurean embodiment of the onset of middle age: the dinner party. Previously if friends came for dinner you'd have contented yourself – and your guests – with a packet of Pringles as a starter and whatever was in the fridge as a main; the wine, or rather plonk, would have been plucked from the special offers section in the local supermarket, with no attention to the grape or vintage. Quantity not quality was the dish of the day back then, and if you could tell what colour the wine was when the lights were low, you were considered something of an expert.

As for dessert, well, this was definitely the main attraction. Remember? Nope, I don't mean a home-made raspberry and white chocolate Italian trifle, hand-crafted lemon meringues or a tasty fruit cobbler that you lovingly prepared over several hours (or days). I mean you thought it the height of sophistication to whack three ice-cubes in a glass (pint glass of course) and fill it to the brim with Baileys. *Et voilà*. A delicious, and – more importantly – alcoholic, pudding!

Table manners were also essential at such dos. But not the kind you consider so important now (i.e. using a knife and fork, a napkin, the right glass and the like). Rather, teenage and twenty-something etiquette dictated that the spliff was passed from left to right, that you inhaled for at least three seconds, and that nobody hogged it for too long! If your tastes were even Class A-er (see what I did there?), then the host or hostess had to have first dibs, or the guests would be asked to leave. Throwing up during the dinner party was okay so long as you held your hands up to it (hmm, which was possibly quite hard when you were clutching on to the toilet rim). If your guests informed you they'd thrown up the next day, they were not accusing you of poisoning them (unless you count alcohol poisoning) but were giving you the thumbs up for having plied them with so much drink. Indeed food came last in a long line of other priorities: did your guest have fun? Did they pull? Will your party be the talk of the town for months?

Now, despite a nagging feeling that it's just what Mum would have done, you plan the menu at the same time as you send out the invitations – that is, a month before the bash itself, flicking through your cookery books with the earnestness of a general about to lay siege at some great battle. Irish stew, cheese fondue, or cordon bleu? Decisions! Decisions! Having settled on your menu, you write the shopping list; planning a visit to the butcher, the baker and, what the heck, the candlestick maker (soft lighting will be so much more soothing for your guests, some of whom will appreciate the chance for a quick doze) two days in advance, just in case they run out of anything.

Before that little adventure, perhaps a week prior to the main event, your worries turn to the hovel that is your home and you give the house a spring clean. It pays to complement the haute cuisine with a house that's pristine, wouldn't your dear old Mum have said? The night before the bash, glasses, cutlery and crockery are wiped clean (with vinegar, natch) and polished in the morning, to give them that extra sparkle. Now where did I get that idea from, you muse, smug at having called to mind such a useful top-tip? Then it slowly dawns on you, as her voice rings out clear as if she was standing right next to you, "Wipe once to clean, and once to polish." From your Mum, that's where! It's better to be honest. You can't help replicating her little hints and tips can you? Laying the table the night before the party, place cards, hand-crafted centrepiece and artfully folded napkins, and all… She *would* be pleased! Although even she may think recreating the death scene from *Swan Lake* excessive.

IS IT A DELIA?

All that's left on your timetable of self-torture is the cooking. Like the get-together itself this has been organized to within an inch of its life, and woe betide if anything goes wrong! But if it does, say if the odd veg or two drops on the floor, you'd rather dust it off than not offer that all important side-dish, thinking, "it's only a bit of dirt" and invoking the three-second rule. From the very rulebook of she whom you are trying not to mimic.

When the guests are on their way you treat yourself to *another* G & T to steady the old nerves, and put a bit of lippy on to look the part. Only, when you look in the mirror at your alcohol-flushed face, it's your Mother you see tittering tipsily back at you; just like her, you're becoming a martyr to the cause of amusing your mates...

Oh well. It's just that you're not sure you even *like* your friends that much anymore!

You're not sure if you much like being a dinner party guest either. Here, you fret about how to politely show your face, make a contribution to the latest heated debate *and* manage to get back home in time for the new season of *ER*! Then there's the problem of what to take with you.

As a happy-go-lucky young lass you got by on simply turning up – everybody liked having you around and you liked being there. Not now. Instead, you overcompensate for the fact that you don't-actually-want-to-be-there-that-much really, taking a bottle of fizz, one of white and one of red, to show your willingness to take part in the festivities. You just hope the hosts will have the good sense to put the bottles aside for another day. You'll be sticking to the one glass, thanks very much. Busy day tomorrow!

'TIS THE SEASON TO BE JOLLY!

In fact the only time you really drink to excess nowadays – aside from children's parties – is at Yuletide. Not because you will be partying into the night with the rest of them, but simply to see you through the nightmare that is hosting Christmas Day. Because if social events and dinner parties are becoming nothing more than an adult version of show and tell, then Christmas is the icing on the – home-made, of course – cake of your social calendar, the event where you can really show what you're made of and capable of making too: from home-made decorations, the Christmas cake and even wrapping paper, you now like to add the extra special personal touch… your dear old Mum would be proud!

Not that your Christmas plans started with the home-made goodies. No, you'd already been thinking about the big day when you planned your Christmas gift list back in July. So, as you pootle about the beaches of Spain, Portugal or wherever it is you holiday these days – and it's increasingly likely it'll be on the shores of "good old Blighty" – you pick up the odd souvenir that will make a lovely present for Uncle Fred or Aunty Sue. In fact, your Xmas extravaganza started even earlier this year… you'd already bought this year's Christmas cards for a song on Boxing Day!

'Tis the season to be jolly well prepared, eh Mum? Feels good doesn't it? Lying in wait, like a predator stalking its prey, sure that soon you'll be able to pounce with an, "Aha, you see spending three precious hours of our holiday in that flea-ridden, burning hot, Moroccan bazaar was not such a waste of time, was it?"

"This isn't my idea of Boxing day bargain hunting."

Quite right too. Since it's quite usual for someone to pop their head up at the 11th hour (that is, at 11pm on Xmas Eve) filled with sherry, mince pies, and a palpable sense of panic, yelling, "Anybody got any wrapping paper?" or "Oh no! I forgot to buy Dad a present!" Let's face it, you just love the chance to then haughtily produce reams of shiny paper, bought in the sales last year for this very purpose, as well as one of three choices of male presents (you just knew they'd come in handy), tut-tutting that classic Mum saying: "There's always one!"

The magic of Christmas? The mania of Christmas, more like. If your Ghost of Christmas Past paid you a visit, she'd be the one that was spooked: "where has that party girl gone?" she'd think; the one who danced on tables at the office Christmas do, and didn't worry about who'd clear up the mess if something got spilt? The one who liked nothing more than to go to Midnight Mass on Christmas Eve... and then on to a party? Look no further than 10pm on Christmas Day, when, after a few sherries too many, you start up a family sing-song on the kids' karaoke machine or get out your favourite festive records and try to get everyone dancing. Who else could be so embarrassing but your Mum? Perhaps it's time to turn in...

Yes, come along Mum, off to bed with you, it's been a long year of wining and dining... and those discounted Christmas cards and wrapping paper won't buy themselves tomorrow, you know!

Chapter 7

Many A Mickle Makes A Muckle

Let's now examine another everyday life factor which will provide us with yet more tangible evidence that you are turning into your Mum: a relationship so complex that it has given you bigger headaches down the years than those difficult romantic liaisons we spoke about before – and that's your relationship with money.

Looking back to youthful exuberance and extravagance, you had a love-hate relationship with the green stuff. You loved to spend it and hated it when you didn't have any! You wouldn't have thought twice about spending your entire month's salary in a week, or using your last few quid to buy a "must-have" pair of shoes to complete the third new outfit you'd simply had to acquire that month. You spent money like water – or perhaps a more apt liquid to use in this simile would be, you spent money like alcopops as you wasted hours and your hard-earned cash down the pub getting wasted.

Not any more. In today's world, the credit and store cards that used to bulk out your purse have been replaced by one of the most pernicious symbols of the modern supermarket's dominance: the loyalty card. Now you calculate the value of your shopping not only in the money you spend, but in the Nectar points "earned" at the supermarket and petrol station. "Just think", you say to hubbie, rubbing your hands together in a Scrooge-like way. "Next week being Xmas we can accumulate bonus points." Not that you'll ever spend them! Better to wait. Why, you never know what goodies the supermarket might offer if you hold onto the points. Yeah, right! By the time you come to spend them, there won't be any supermarkets, just a government agency responsible for nutrition who feeds us all remotely via giant, robotic straws.

"I'll be alright.... I get withdrawal symtoms."

As you advance in years and your bank balance grows, you start to look at the other side of the, well, coin. Money and possessions come to lose the glitzy, glamorous appeal they had in your heyday: you are becoming Spartan where you once were a spendthrift, and decide (like Bob Dylan) that money doesn't talk, it swears... Your previous zest for life is replaced by a fondness for frugality, summed up by your new catchphrase, smugly churned out wherever appropriate: "Reduce, reuse, repair and recycle!"

WASTE NOT, WANT NOT

If you want concrete evidence of your habitual pooh-poohing of profligacy, we only need sift through your rubbish bin. No, I'm not barking mad. Any celebrity reporter or paparazzo will tell you that a star's trashcan holds more secrets of its owner's lifestyle than a probing in-depth interview could ascertain. As for your rubbish bin's contents, well, we'd have to start by narrowing things down to which bin we're talking about, wouldn't we?

For starters, you have different coloured bins for the different waste in the house; the red bin for all non-recyclable goods, green for tin cans, blue for paper, brown for bottles and so on. It goes without saying that each of these has been rinsed. Wouldn't want the bin men to think you're *dirty*, would you – or for there to be any signs of, um, waste, in the waste bin!

As for food wastage, well, there isn't any, is there? Indeed the lack of it is a tell-tale sign that the penny has finally

107

dropped on your own mother's cries of "waste not, want not!" Rather than merrily slinging out leftovers from the evening meal, you chide those who've left your roast-beef flavoured sorbet untouched (that Heston Blumenthal has a lot to answer for) with, "There are starving children in Africa, you know!" ("Yeah, and there'll be starving children in Bolton," they might well reply with unworldly-wise selfishness, "if you keep feeding us this muck.")

We could now crown you Queen of the Leftovers, as you boil up endless smelly dead carcasses to fill your freezer with various "useful" stocks and sauces. Well done you, invoking that gung-ho war-time spirit of eating every single morsel or scrap! Err, but weren't you born way after rationing ended?

Who cares? It's fun to stockpile supplies as if food was going out of style and dream wistfully about owning a larder — a larder filled with practical tinned products or those with a long shelf-life, that is. Well, you never know when they'll come in handy! This also allows you to indulge your love for bargain hunting and buying value packs or two-for-three offers on everything — as well as earning those precious extra points on your loyalty card. So what if nobody in the family eats oxtail soup? It's flavour of the month, literally. Thanks, Mum!

Even if you complained when your own Mother did it in the past, you've begun to eat perishable goods when they are well past their sell-by date. So, should the bread look like it's got stilton spread all over the crust or if the milk has taken on the appearance of glue, you simply shrug your shoulders, and mutter with an insane look in your eye, "It's only a bit of mould," or "It's only just on the turn!" Quite right too. The mouldier, the smellier, the better, and the more self-righteous you feel. Should your *famille* come down with a strange tummy bug, it's never down to drinking milk that looks like yoghurt. No way! Rather you blame it on the evil ready-made pudding they conned you into buying.

"We've been together for 12 years now. I think it's time we thought seriously about composting."

And what very few measly scraps of food you do resignedly send to their grave (never an early one though – keep up!), you will throw on your newly acquired compost heap. Rarely are you happier than when making a trip to the bottom of the garden to dispose of apple peelings (assuming you haven't used them to make some strange, crunchy apple sauce) and you're darned near ecstatic when you go an ecological step further and invest in a wormery!

My gosh. You'd sign up for meals on wheels given half the chance, wouldn't you? What am I talking about? Course you wouldn't. No, not because you're only about half the pensionable age and you're not allowed them yet, but because you're too darned stingy to pay for food where the cost of every single ingredient can't be traced.

That doesn't make for a very pleasant experience when you dine out does it? Dine out? Don't make me laugh! Whereas once the opportunity not to cook would have been top of your wish-list, it now features highly on your "don't wish" list (somewhere between talking dirty and smoking grass). A few reasons. Firstly, who knows how clean the kitchens are? (FYI: you can usually tell by checking the state of the loos. Fact!) Secondly, thirdly, fourth, etc., etc., *ad infinitum*, because you're too darned tight!

On special occasions you might, however, be found munching away in the local bistro, but you inspect the bill so closely, the waiter wonders if you're examining it to see if it's edible. Just pay the £1.50 for the coffees and be done with it, you old whingebag! And don't forget to leave a handsome tip.

WERE YOU BORN IN BARN?

Your growing penchant for penny-pinching is not limited to the kitchen (yours or anyone else's) by any means! If we took a tour of your home we'd find countless instances of your compunction over your previous life of over-consumption. Walls, doors and windows are well insulated, and if anyone claims to be feeling the cold, instead of turning up the heating, you fix them with a frosty glare and declare icily, "Well, put another jumper on then!" Then, should they leave the door open as they shuffle, shivering, upstairs to collect said garment, you can churn out another of your eco-friendly catchphrases, "Close that door – were you born in a barn?"

Casting our eye further around the house, another room where we will find you saving energy as well as water is the bathroom. In past times you might have luxuriated in the bath for hours, possibly even showering afterward to rinse off! Not now. Instead you decree bathtime a weekly treat – showers are so much more environmentally friendly. (And save you a few pence on the old water bills, eh?) As if this was not enough to embarrass the kids, you strike a crushing blow to the self-consciousness of youth with a sign hanging over the loo saying: "If it's yellow let it mellow, if it's brown flush it down." A sign which not in so many words says, "Help! I'm turning into my Mum!"

For it was she who taught you that wasting water is as close as you'll ever come to making the baby Jesus himself cry. Just think back to her stomping about the house, yelling "There's a water shortage, you know" the minute anybody turned on a tap. (Sure, there is a world-wide water shortage, but growing up in Glasgow it was not something you'd notice.)

111

"Mother... I'm calling health and safety if you don't get rid of the water meter."

Time to visit the bedroom where it's more than likely that you have begun to line your bottom drawer with an impressive collection of freebies – miniature toiletries picked up in hotels, for instance. Well, you might get away with giving dotty Aunty Sue the best of them for her birthday, you think, stingily. After all, what's she ever given you, apart from the occasional headache?

Such gratefulness for gratis goodies does not end there. Your favourite freebies are the great newspaper give-aways so popular these days and you make a sterling effort to get hold of every single wall-chart, DVD or CD on offer. So what if you hate *Tubular Bells* or have seen *Black Beauty* a million times – "Never look a gift horse in the mouth!" you say, whilst buying a newspaper which no-one will ever read and which will swiftly end up in the neatly arranged recycling box. (The blue one, for paper, of course – remember)?

MAKE DO AND MEND

In fact, if you could help it, you wouldn't pay for anything. But if you must, you certainly won't pay much. Why bother when you can mend stuff or buy it second-hand? Suddenly you have become the domestic equivalent of a doctor in the hospital drama, refusing to give up on any household item until it's definitely, absolutely dead. As such, you buy into all sorts of weird and wonderful theories about giving the dishwasher an aspirin if it goes on the blink or defibrillating a dodgy hoover, as you shout "clear" to your increasingly embarrassed kiddies!

Of all household items, clothing is your favourite for making do and mending. "What is it with this throwaway generation," you mutter, "buying cheap clothes from Primark or Top Shop which need replacing every couple of months?" Still, you'd have to admit, you admire their "keen" prices and have been known to shop there now and then in an attempt to keep up youthly appearances. However, as you acquire your middle-aged sea legs, unlike the younger generation, should said clothes rip or get holes under the arms, you'll be sure to darn, stick or sew them, to make them good as new.

And if something can't be fixed, you'd rather "do without" or put up with dodgy gadgets and holey clobber. Better to watch a fuzzy telly or do the dishes by hand than invest in a pricy new electrical appliance. Sadly, you'll no doubt come up against mounting pressure from your gadget-obsessed family. What to do but give everyone a lecture on today's throw-away society before heading reluctantly for Comet or some such electrical superstore. (All the while breathing a small sigh of relief. I mean, if there was no telly you'd to have to come up with some other way to keep them entertained.)

Arriving at the store, you feel more out of your depth than a toddler at a Mensa convention. "What is all this gobbledegook about these gadgets?" you moan. "And what's the difference between analogue and digital again?" Then, as you finally settle on a rather minute and old-fashioned looking TV set, you look at the price-tag and holler, "How much?" at the spotty 17-year-old sales-assistant. ("Nice one", thinks the assistant, "showing which generation you're from there!" You can always tell the mums are in town when that question's asked.)

"Cheer up. It's not every day that your father and I treat ourselves to a meal out."

SAVING FOR A RAINY DAY

Doing without, as described, means for the first time in your life you have surplus money in the bank. But do you spend it? Do you go for broke and book a few well-earned weeks in the Caribbean? Do you get the urge to splurge and head for the personal shopping department at Harvey Nicks? Do you heck as like! It's an undeniable signal that you're holding up a white flag to the onslaught of your middle years when the more money you accrue, the less you spend. It's as if you fear now you've got it, it'll grow legs, decide it doesn't like you any more and find someone more interesting to hang out with!

Cripes. It's hardly surprising it finds you so dull, what with your increasing fondness for financial accounting – it never gets to go anywhere! For the truth of the matter is, you're now as miserly as you once were wasteful. Back in the spendthrift days, any bank statement that dropped through your letterbox had a life expectancy of about five minutes before you threw it in the bin. Bills were treated with a similar contempt, and you wouldn't have dreamt of even looking at them until you knew the angry red one had arrived.

Now each bank statement and bill will probably outlive the family pet, as you catalogue each one in a ring-binder, specially ordered from the bank. As if this was not ghastly enough, you check your bank statements against what's on your cheque stubs and note down every single penny you spend. As you do so, you shudder in recognition of your Mum's "good housekeeping". Uh-oh! For my, um, money there is little you can do but admit that such cost-consciousness signals you're becoming just like her...

"Never mind," you harrumph, "my monetary meticulousness augurs well for the years ahead." Yes it does, dear, and just as well really. You have become obsessed by your financial future, day-dreaming endlessly about your lifestyle in retirement. Even if it's 30 years away! "But hold on," you yell, "I object! I've thought about a pension before." Yeah, sure you did, but – a bit like death – when you did so in the past, you supposed that they were necessary evils that only happened to other people.

But, as the thought of retirement sneaks up on you at an alarming rate, you remember the statistics about one in three marriages ending in divorce and having to look after yourself in old age. Hmm, the way your husband is increasingly getting on your nerves, singledom in old age seems increasingly possible, so you stop just *thinking* about pensions and take decisive action about *getting* one.

You also frequently bring to mind your Mum's advice about saving for a rainy day. And, my goodness, you must have an apocalyptically bleak view of future weather patterns the amount you are putting to one side! Not content with simply setting up an appropriate savings account, you take the sensible step of consulting a financial adviser to talk the talk on PEPs and ISAs. As you walk away from this meeting, you get a self-satisfied thrill, and think, "I should have done this years ago!" It brings to mind the kick you used to get from spending, from spunking all your wages on a spontaneous weekend away, or the pleasure you once felt form going on an all-day shopping spree. Who'd have thought all it took to regain youthful exuberance was a quick chat with the bank manager?

Sure, you stepped over your bank manager's threshold in the past, but previously you relished it about as much as you would being thrown to the lions – it was hardly *your* idea to discuss your burgeoning bank loans. But there comes a time when you begin to visit such financial wheelers and dealers of your own volition – and what's more actually look forward to having a good old chinwag about your financial affairs. It's moments like this when you realize there's no going back, and it's good common-sense all the way for you now!

Mind you, even if you did get a windfall from the afore-mentioned savings and investments, it's not likely you'd spend any of your rapidly escalating wealth. As we've seen throughout this chapter you're far too much of a tight-wad these days. So if the kids approach you for a loan, taking you for their personal banker, you wag your finger at them as patronizingly as possible, mumbling, "Neither a borrower nor a lender be!"

Little do they know that half of your savings are in their name and the other half is willed to them on your death! Just like your own parents, you take great pleasure in constantly saying "No!" to your kids, while at the same time secretly squirreling away as much as possible for them. Well, you hope that's what your own Mum's doing, anyway… But, just like her, if your kids ask about this, you say with a humbled look, "Well of course there won't be that much left for you when I'm gone!" As if you were

93, not 38 going on 53! There's no denying it... such self-deprecation and suggestions of being decrepit can only mean one thing. Yes! You want to scream as loudly as possible and to whomever will listen the very title of this book. Come on, all together now!

I can't hear you – don't be shy. There's no shame in admitting it. No shame either in coming clean about the money-saving tips and tricks you've picked up from her. Buy your kids bubbles to blow at parties? Nope, just get an empty shampoo bottle and put in a dash of Fairy Liquid. Shampoo? Pah! Oatmeal on dry hair does the trick nicely. Really? But it gets worse. Now, like she did, you keep every scrap of soap and mould them together with a little glycerine to make a new bar. I give up! Scrooge has got nothing on you, or on your Mum for that matter!

Chapter 8

Everything Just So!

Everybody knows – especially your Mum – that you "learn from your mistakes" and boy, did you put this maxim to the test in your younger years. Fashion, finance and fooling around were key areas that got you in a muddle, and when you were a little older you became pretty good at fouling up your professional and family lives too.

Think back to erroneous events of the past, and your reaction to them. Did you let them get you down? Nope, you took on board Mum's remark that "a smile costs less than a frown", and didn't give a tinker's toot if you japed things up too much. Slept with your best friend's fella? Oh well, doing her a favour, weren't you, letting her know what a scumbag he was? Threw up on your boss at the work Xmas party? Never mind. You weren't so keen on a career in law, anyway. Left your hair dye on too long and ended up with light-green locks? Well, you always did want to be a trend-setter.

Blunders don't wash over you so readily any longer. In fact now you'd rather not make another one again (or own up to one). Everything has to be "just so" and your attitude is "perfection, nothing less," leading to a permanent state of agitation as well as of perfection! My goodness, no wonder you've become a tad neurotic, having become so pernickety about people and possessions. Living up to your own high standards has become a worry for you, never mind for your loved ones. In fact especially for your loved ones as your method for dealing with this anxiety is to become a control freak!

EVERYTHING HAS IT'S PLACE

Of all your controlling behaviour there is one outburst that doubtless annoys those in earshot of you more than any other. Your nearest and dearest may put up with no end of criticisms and complaints, all manner of advice and admonishments, endless ear-bashings and tongue-lashings, but perhaps the one which will trouble them the most is the irrefutably annoying "Everything has its place!"

Now remind me, were you born at the turn of the last century or somewhere in the latter half? Such is your fussiness and finickiness, anyone would think you wanted to hark back to a time when children could be seen, not heard… and were most definitely inactive. Because nothing rattles your cage more than when you look for the good scissors to find they have been used for an inappropriate activity, like opening a tin of paint, or craftwork.

That could be why you've become so obsessed by putting everything "where it belongs" and allocating special places, drawers and cupboards for particular items in the house. But hold on. Do you let on to anyone else who shares your abode where these special places are? Some chance! You prefer instead to stash sticky tape, sticking-plasters and other such useful bits and pieces in darkened corners of the home and then delight in producing them, when asked, as if you were a magician plucking a rabbit out of a hat! Your kids look on with the bored guise of the magician's assistant. They've seen the same trick performed countless times before, and with the same inevitable result: they get blamed for the item going missing in the first place.

"If he could trace the matching sock I've 25 or 30 to account for."

How was anyone else to know that the sewing kit "lives" in an old ice-cream tub in the linen cupboard? Or that the sticky tape is in with the tea towels? Or that everybody's passports are in the sock drawer? Who cares? If you told them, you'd miss out on that enormous satisfaction of producing said item and proclaiming: "See! Where it always is!"

Your exacting standards about household apparatus don't stop there. Not only does everything have to be found where you left it, but you begin to keep a well-stocked home, prepared for any household mishap or misadventure. Like an army quartermaster getting kitted up for battle, no budding Mum worth her salt can be seen dead without the correct appurtenances and equipment.

Sewing kit? Yes, Ma'am! Tool kit? Medical kit? Yes, Ma'am! Each kit being filled to the brim with the odds and sods you now deem crucial to your family's survival. I mean, imagine if a button fell off little Jemima's best dress and you didn't have the right-coloured thread to sew it back on. Disaster! Consider the heinous situation, should there not be any Savlon in the house when young Emily bumps her knee. Catastrophe! What if you had to change a plug and the tool kit was missing the right kind of screwdriver to do so? Well, it just doesn't bear thinking about, does it?

What's that, I hear you snigger? You think I've forgotten something. But no, I saved the best for last. I know full well that there's another kit you keep hidden from the rest of the family – the stationery kit. Here you keep all manner of notelets, thank you and birthday cards. Why, you'd come out in hives if the right greeting card was not available to send at the right time.

FUNKY JUNK

Another sign that you're becoming more anxious is your new tendency to hoard. Like a squirrel in the autumn months, you just can't help storing away useful stuff for the long days, weeks, months, and – hell, there's no limit to your future planning – years ahead. Mind you, it's not like you don't accumulate the non-useful stuff as well. You just can't bear to throw anything away?

Don't deny it. You've become the mother of all hoarders haven't you? Why is it that items you'd have probably deemed useless in the past are accruing more value than the crown jewels? Empty yoghurt pots, old newspapers, plastic carrier bags are all put aside with the thought that they might just come in useful one day. What possible use could they be? Some bizarre nuclear winter where humanity is driven to making yoghurt pot walkie-talkies in order to survive? A famine where we have to eat the crusty remains at the bottom of tins of paint? "Well, yes", you spit out dramatically, "whyever not?!"

Another of your favoured items to stockpile is the memento from your early years, the thing that makes you sigh with fondness and through rose-tinted spectacles at those cherished and girlish childhood moments. So, photos, trinkets and school reports are all spared the bin; your exam revision, school and swimming certificates all laugh in the face of the dustman's evil grasp. Not that you ever really look at them, but you're filled with sentimental certainty that your kids will want to thoroughly peruse them some day. Sure! Just like you take an interest in your own Mum's childhood memories and possessions!

"And the present owners have fully insulated
the loft."

Speaking of kids, you can't stop yourself amassing burgeoning amounts of their stuff either, can you? Clothes, toys, books – you name it! Yeah, you name it, then you label it, bag it and bung it in the loft. Well, hubbie does keep refusing that vasectomy, so you never know. And even if you've no immediate plans for procreation, there's only another decade or so till grandchildren come along. The would-be Mum also takes on the misguided notion that keeping hold of the clothes of her youth will be appreciated by her female progeny in years to come (or the male ones; nobody could accuse you of being old-fashioned in that regard!). And so you put aside items that you can only dream of fitting back into as hand-me-downs for your daughter. Lucky her! I'm certain that in 2020 early 1990s Betty Boo-style catsuits are going to be all the rage. Not!

Even when moving house you cling onto your tasteless and treasured possessions. And what you do get rid of, you don't give away lightly. Sure, you could do a good turn and take those barely worn kiddy clothes along to Oxfam. But, well, it's so much more fun to try and make some cash from your, um, cache of old clobber and collectables. And so you participate in that weekly activity that righteous and goodly citizens the country over take part in with an almost holy dose of dedication every Sunday morning. Church? No, silly! The car boot sale.

Get your motor running and head out on the highway. (Not too fast though!) Life couldn't get any more rock 'n' roll than this, could it? You'd think so, the kick you get out off whizzing down an A road, before first light, ready to flog a random collection of tat to some poor suckers. Only, upon arrival, you discover that said tat is not quite as abundant as when you packed the car last night. What happened to the boxful of '70s *Men and Motors* magazines (eh, Dad?), why did the world's most lovingly tended *My Little Pony* collection fall out the back of the trunk (daughter), and where the hell's that ugly Toby Jug Aunt Bessie bought you last Xmas? Errr, well admit it Mum, she is your favourite auntie so you felt a little mean selling it. Back in the cupboard with you, Uncle Toby!

Here comes an irony though: what happens on your return from the car boot or jumble sale? Is your car boot any lighter than when you set out at the crack of dawn to get the best spot? Course it's not. You just couldn't resist that 1985 edition of the *Jackie Annual* poking out at you from the car next door, you've always hankered after a 1950s coat rack – and that anthology of the collected works of Shakespeare (minus *Twelfth Night* and *Much Ado About Nothing*... well, you prefer the tragedies anyway!) was a billy-bargain at £1.50!

It's time to bring you up-to-date lady and let you in on something. There's a magical world where people can buy and sell stuff without getting up at the crack of dawn, or glumly sipping cups of cold tea in the rain. Never heard of it? The world-wide web, the internet, a network that links you to other people, and more importantly to other people's goods? Alright, alright. I'm being facetious. But did it never occur to you, you'd have more luck poncing your wares on ebay than slogging your guts out in the corner of a muddy field? Oh, I see! Afraid of cyber and identity theft. Sheesh. Just another new-fangled modern invention to stress you out!

EVERYTHING BUT THE KITCHEN SINK

For further evidence that you're becoming a bit of a worry-wart we only need think about all the accoutrements we lug about with us on a daily basis. It's hardly surprising that Mums up and down the land are often accused of dragging everything but the kitchen sink with them here, there and everywhere, when we take a moment to consider the handbag. The handbag! Iconic cultural symbol that has woman written all over it. Yes, the lowly handbag is a tangible reminder that you have become a hoarder extra-ordinaire in the manner of your Mother.

I mean, how many magazine articles have you read that suggest you can read a person's personality by looking at the contents of their handbags? Actually, put it another way, 'cause I credit you with more intelligence than to actually read those pathetic pieces – how many magazine articles have been written about how you can read a person's personality by looking at the contents of their handbags? Millions, let me tell you. So let's try this out for size. What kind of woman's handbag contains the following items: pocket hankies (two packs), mints, paracetemol, baby wipes, Rennies, lipstick, purse, brolly, tampons, bus time-table, reams of receipts. Hmm, let's think. No condoms, no miniature vodkas, no little black book. This does not point us towards the single girl about town. No fancy leather filofax, no groovy blackberry, no hand-embossed business cards with the "Ms" carved in gold leaf. Okay, not the handbag of a feisty young professional either then. Nor that of a student with its lack of flyers, concert tickets and assortment of differently coloured pens. I'm scoobied, I really am, I mean just who would have a handbag like this?

"I'm not sure what that handbag says about you!"

Okay, I'll stop now; you and I both know it's glaringly obvious. It's the handbag of a Mum. And not just any Mum. Look a little closer. Yup, that half-munched low-calorie chocolate bar gives it away – it's yours! (By the way, what eejit dreamt up that sadistic little number? Looks like chocolate, smells like chocolate, tastes like ****)

Not content with filling your handbag with decidedly sensible contents, remembering your dear old Mum's own accessory habit, you decide that you must own one kind of handbag for every occasion. What are you like? In your twenties you didn't fetishize leather like you do now (and if you did, it was probably kinky). Nope, in your salad days you made do with a daytime handbag, a shopping bag and an evening bag. Now we'd need nearly a herd of cows to come up with the (leather) goods to sate your appetite for accessories!

Don't worry, I'm sure you'll find a use for them when you go on holiday. For now the old saying "everything but the kitchen sink" comes into its own. I mean, is it really necessary to take four pieces of luggage for a two-day mini-break? Yet, you approach the task of packing with such relish, your husband wonders if you've got a bloke as well as suitcases stashed in the cupboard.

Packing is important though, isn't it? Wouldn't want to leave anything behind, would we? And so begins your "Russian Doll" version of packing as toilet bags are placed inside carrier bags in case of leakage, placed inside a laundry bag which will come in useful on the return journey, placed in a holdall that you can carry as hand luggage in case anything gets lost *en route*, and finally placed in the suitcase which darn near breaks your back as you put it in the taxi on the way to the airport! Bloody hell and you've broken a nail.

What's that, though? You beg the taxi driver to turn around when you realize that you've forgotten the portable smoke alarm and carbon monoxide kit! Well, quite right too – wouldn't your Mum have remarked, "Better safe than sorry"? Best wang in the smoke alarm, too.

WOMEN ON THE EDGE...

Quite on edge there, aren't we dear? Don't deny it, as the years roll by you're becoming more neurotic by the minute. Let's for instance have a think about your bedtime routine: 11pm. Front door bolted? Check. Back door locked and bolted? Check. Boiler set to timer, all gas hobs off? Check. TV and all other electrical appliances switched off, and NOT on standby? Check. 11.15 pm. Front door bolted? Hang on a mo, I'm getting déjà vu here, you shudder, as you make your way to bed. Nonetheless you pad back downstairs and do your check of the perimeters one more time, just in case memory doesn't serve. What are you thinking? Of course memory doesn't serve. You've reached that stage in life when having a good memory is an increasingly dim and distant, err, memory.

Crawling into bed does not put an end to your bedtime worries and woes. Before you drift off to sleep you catalogue each and every single minor problem you can think of, as if reflecting on them now is going to do you any good. It could be a meeting you're due to have at work tomorrow, it could be the fact your husband has been out on the tiles a little too much recently, it could be that itchy rash you keep getting (are the two perhaps connected, you worry yet further?). And if you wrack your brains and can't find anything to worry about, you worry that you must have forgotten something. There's that rotten memory problem again!

It will come as no surprise, then, even if you're none too delighted about it, that when Neighbourhood Watch come knocking for volunteers, you sign on the dotted line before anyone can say "paranoid meddling busy-body". Such is your predilection toward paranoia, your worries don't stop at your own front door. Indeed, they stretch as far as the end of the street.

Needless to say, it's an omen that you're headed for life as Mum when you don't just join the Neighbourhood Watch but relish the chance to have a nose about, to see what your neighbours are up to. Thus you become more of a nuisance than the very people you're meant to be deterring, and her next door would rather be burglarized than have you pay another visit, torch in hand, tongue-in-cheek, with your faux-fretting, "Everything all right? I heard some *terrible* noises coming from your bedroom just now, banging and all sorts!"

But nosing on passionate parents is nothing compared to how much you spy on the neighbours' kids. Remember when you were little? All the kiddywinks on the street played hopscotch, jump rope and the like until well after the sun went down. Nobody batted an eyelid when children hopped on their bicycles and peddled around and about, as long as they came back in time for tea. Wouldn't it be nice if some of that care-free spirit was granted to today's children? Allow such freedoms to the scallywags of today? Perish the thought! No, instead, you compile a list of the children in the area you deem to be a nuisance. Then, despite a niggle of self-doubt that you're getting old before your time, you bang on number 5's door and have a

"Don't move.... it's the local neighbourhood witch."

30-minute whinge about the "yoof of today", and could their little darlings kindly stop playing football in the street?

Becoming quite the hypocrite about the homestead, aren't we? It's not like you to offer open and out-stretched arms to anybody who knocks on your door, is it? Quite the reverse actually. The fledgling fuddy-duddy has little time or patience for anyone but their extended family or closest circle of friends. And in some cases you blow a gasket if they call uninvited too. Hence, despite a niggling feeling that it makes you not just an old fart but a gasbag full of flatulence, you buy one of those NO CIRCULARS OR HAWKERS signs for your front door. That should keep the preachers, peddlers and politicians at bay!

And yet unwanted visitors don't win the prize for the people who annoy you most. Oh, no; you save a special dose of venomous vociferation for telesales representatives or those who still manage, in the modern age, what with speed-dialling etc, to dial a wrong number. But here comes another paranoid delusion: if they've got my number, what else do they know about me?

Oh dear, the number's truly up on your previous life as a carefree gal when you show such paranoiac tendencies. It's as if you've been bodysnatched; that your brain's been replaced with that of your mother's. Get me with my conspiracy theories! I don't know who's more of a worrier: you, me or your Mum. I'm off for a lie down before I can even think about writing the next chapter.

Chapter 9

There's No Place Like Home

In the days BC – before cleaning – there lived a slatternly young woman who changed her bedclothes once a month, had a stack of dishes in the kitchen sink resembling the leaning tower of Pisa and whose priority was humping, not cushion plumping. Having a "life laundry" meant finally picking up the dirty knickers and chocolate wrappers that had lain under the bed for months, and she was the original inspiration for the phrase, "not getting your hands dirty".

Yes, that insanitary slob was you. Now, as you slowly immerse yourself in the washing up and the murky waters of maturity, you can but reminisce about a time when worries over being spotless meant being acne-free and cleaning up was something you did during a late-night poker session with your mates. Indeed there may be no clearer (or should that be cleaner?) indication that you're headed for life in the slow lane than your changing attitude towards housework.

The first indication of this is the amount of time spent on your daily chores. Or more accurately, if we're talking about the past, let's call these your monthly chores. Back then you didn't have that hereditary compulsion to keep your place spick and span seven days a week and your motto might have been "cleanliness is next to oddliness". Life was quite simply too short and tidying up was a five-minute job, only undertaken if your own Mother was coming round to visit! But you always crossed your fingers that she'd avoid the cupboard under the stairs. Otherwise known as the cupboard of horrors where fags, old mags and rubbish bags were chucked just before she rang the doorbell. Couldn't have you living up to your childhood nickname, could we "Mucky Pup"?

Now you follow a strict timetable for tidying up which must be observed not only by you but by other fed-up family members. Having changed your tune somewhat you decide that "cleanliness is next to godliness" and begin to take this a bit too literally, worshipping at the shrine of Mr Muscle on a daily basis. Your routine starts before everyone else is out of bed as you hoover before breakfast, "just to get things straight", and ends with the washing up as soon as everyone has finished their tea and in some cases – such is your stress about mess – before they've even finished their pudding!

Indeed, the others living in your house could probably chuck out the calendar that hangs on your fridge, and tell which day of the week it is by which cleaning activity you're doing. Wet washing hanging all over the show? Must be Monday! Kitchen floor polished so enthusiastically that the toddler's gone for a burton? It could only be Wednesday!

But the increased woman-hours spent sweating over chores aren't the most significant indication, when it comes to housework, that you're turning into your Mum. Oh no! You may as well throw in the (laundered and ironed) towel and admit you're her domestic doppelganger – when you realize you've started enjoying it!

If there was an award for the world's most perfect house-wife you'd be a leading contender – an honour you aspire to even if you are a single woman, living alone! "Thank God for global warming," you are often to be found thinking guiltily, "I can start my spring-cleaning in January!" Not that you need an excuse to start sprucing up your abode... go on get out the Marigolds.

IF YOU CAN'T STAND THE HEAT... GET IN THE KITCHEN

The epicentre of this new-found love of all things homely has to be the kitchen – the heart of every home, as is often said. Here you will find yourself doing, saying and, above all, baking, things that conjure up images of all things maternal. If you want proof, let's think firstly about your kitchen's layout.

"I've no idea what it does but it's our No.1 best seller."

When you were a spring chicken, the most important items to be found in the kitchen were the bottle opener and the microwave oven into which you wanged your lonely ready meals for one. Now you're a regular at your local kitchenware shop – in fact the store detective wonders if you might be shop-lifting to order, such is the frequency of your visits! Your kitchen drawers are now crammed full of a variety of gleaming and menacing-looking utensils that fill a variety of tasks: apple corers, strawberry de-seeders and pastry-cutters to name but a superfluous few. In fact you've so many of the darned things, when you come across one in the drawer, you forget which purpose it actually serves!

How did this happen, that you became such a home-body, with the smell of home-baked goods – quiches, pies and cakes – wafting around your home with startling regularity? And, that, if you are not *actually* baking, you are drooling over recipe books, thinking about which next flavoursome treat to try out next? How could it be that you relish the chance to don a pinny, and flourish the rolling pin with glee and aplomb, ready for a cake-making fest extraordinaire?

Probably – let's be honest – it's not because you're trying to fatten up the family, or love to dish out sweet treats, but because it's the only room in the house where you can find a bit of peace and quiet, or listen to *The Archers* or Radio 2 without any interruption!

Small wonder then, that when the little cherubs descend on your self-imposed solitary confinement, you visibly bristle. And that when they ask that phrase that parents the world-over dread beyond any other, "What's for dinner?", you churn out a variation on a traditional Mum answer. Now, depending on how politely you've been brought up yourself or how many times you've been asked that particular question that week, your answer may vary between simply "Food!" or, "Bread and water," or if you have been driven to complete distraction and can't sublimate your rage, the rather naughty, "**** with sugar on it!" God, that felt good, you think, why didn't I get this off my chest before!

As we've established, at home you are truly the lady of the manor and – to upgrade your noble status – it's in the kitchen that you are queen of all you survey. Hence this is the spot in the house where you can really go to town with the classic Mum sayings your family will be coming to know and dread. In this room, you're beginning to reel them out with almost no pause for breath, with a repertoire ranging from the time-worn, "Eat your greens!" to "Crusts will make your hair curl" to the outright lie, "Carrots will help you see in the dark." That'll teach them to encroach on your turf!

QUEEN OF THE CASTLE

It's also in the kitchen that we will find you most at home, day-dreaming over one of your Mum's, and now your, favoured subjects – home improvements. As previously mentioned, you no longer chit-chat with girlfriends into the wee small hours, sat at the kitchen table brooding and boozing the night away over tales of failed or funked relationships. Now there's nothing you like better than to discuss Agas, rather than the sagas surrounding the ups and downs of your love lives.

"Doing up the kitchen" (or bathroom, hallway, bedroom – anywhere really that could be home-improved: stripped and dipped, basically taken apart and put together again) becomes an obsession. You'd probably not even balk at paying the same for a granite worktop that you used to earn in a year in your first job. Sourcing such marvels becomes a source of great joy – and great stress. Indeed, the writing's on the (tastefully papered) wall for the heady days of youth when your maritals aren't over any passionate misdemeanour but in the wallcoverings aisle at B & Q!

There's no better indication of this new-found love for all things homely than your changing magazine consumption. Some time ago you may have given up *Cosmo* for the more grown-up *Elle* or *Grazia* but now, as you become more like your Mum, it's more than likely you'll want to do away with fashion and sex tips completely, and swap them for home deco tips. So, you heave a comfortable sigh as you cancel your subscription to *Glamour* magazine (it's finally dawned on you each issue is recycled bi-annually anyway) and sign up to your new middle-aged reads of *Homes and Gardens* and *Good Housekeeping*.

Now, instead of drooling over photos of Brad Pitt or Johnny Depp in their latest flicks, you can get hot under the collar over the latest soft furnishing offerings from Cath Kidston or Laura Ashley. Just what is it about you and soft furnishings these days? Yes, you might have had throws in your apartments when you were single – but that was usually to cover up the stains on your second-hand sofa. Now, as you and your partner climb into bed, it's anybody's guess how long it will take you to fight your way through the huge piles of quilts and cushions. Whoops – that particularly furry one was your husband's stomach!

Home decorating now takes up so much of your free time, you wonder if you should audition for *Property Ladder* even though you've no immediate plans to move out. Thing is, though, by the time you have each room in the house picture-perfect, you decide to make that move, after all. How else will you spend your free time once you've finished your home makeover? Here's an idea. I think you'll like it. Why not spend your free time surfing the net to see how far your home improvements have pushed up the price of your property? Silly me. It goes without saying this is an activity you already undertake on a weekly basis. Ooh, look! That three-bedroom maisonette down the road sold for 50% more than they paid for it. But, oh no! The credit crunch has struck and – horror of horrors – prices are going down as well as up. Should we move now while the going's pretty good, or wait for interest rates to come down, inflation to go up? Help! You're turning into a property bore. Help! You're turning into your Mum!

Don't sulk. It's true. Especially when you start to contemplate the ultimate signal that you've reached new heights of wannabe Mum-ness. And that's when you consider buying a second property. Whether it's a *pied-à-terre* in sunny Suffolk, a rambling château (err, ruin) in the Dordogne or an 'investment property' in the Balkans, you can't deny that getting in a state about real estate is a contender for the prize of the topmost sign that middle-age is but a hop, skip and a jump away!

"Whether you should or shouldn't audition for *'Property Ladder'* isn't really within my remit!"

IRONING OUT A FEW PROBLEMS

We have now established that the submission to your inner Domestic Goddess is cast-iron proof that you are yielding to the inevitable and morphing into your Mum. And while we're on the subject of irons, what about your new approach to ironing itself?

"I'm guessing it's not a surfboard."

Why, when we're about to make the leap from youth to the grey-hued land of middle age, do we start to iron anything and everything, including towels, sheets, hankies and our – increasingly sensible – pants? A far cry from the time when you checked whether every item was "crease-free"! Now you spend hours in front of the telly brandishing your iron, humming along gaily to some sappy soap or, worse still, the *Countdown* music! No such care-and-crease-free days now!

It's as if you were waiting your whole life to become a laundry mistress: what was once a weekly or fortnightly activity has become as second-nature as sleeping – or breathing in or out! What's more, you split the laundry with more scientific exactitude than splitting the atom, as the wash load is sorted into brights, whites, lights, darks and delicates. You're smug as you do so, thinking how gleaming white and pristine little Johnny and Sally's PE shirts will be, and as you do you hum a little ditty your own Mum used to say, "Mix black and white and you'll look a fright." Oh dear. You never thought you'd hear yourself say this, but – by golly, she was right! Just look at those children at Number 6 in their manky grey gym kit!

You wonder if it was also she who bore you (as in gave birth to you, although I am sure the other meaning could fit here too) who suggested that bleach is the housewife's best friend. In a telling re-enactment of her own bedtime routine, you now bleach your cups, the dishcloths and of course bung a quick splash down the loo too before you hit the hay, just to keep everything sanitary. So, as you roll into bed and turn to give your husband a bedtime kiss, he recoils, startled, and harumphs, "God, are you wearing the same perfume as your Mother?"

But perhaps, in spite of your high standards, your inner slob still beats your inner slogger and you still can't bring yourself to do the cleaning. Whatever's to be done? You can't have her next door making you eat dirt for being, erm, dirty. So, what do you do? Hire a cleaner of course. You have to feel sorry for the person that you employ, though! For some reason, as soon as you take on "hired help", you become excessively exacting, wiping your finger across picture rails, ornaments and the like that you would never have dreamt of dusting before.

And who else but your Mum will notice such a thing when she comes to visit, fair boiling over with delight when she sees how well she has taught you in the ways of wiping up!

Not that you escape cleaning entirely when taking on a maid to your dirty work. Because even if you haven't got the time or energy to do it usually, it doesn't take a genius to guess what you do before the cleaner arrives – why, clean up of course! Making hiring a cleaner about as sensible as cutting your own fringe before heading to the hairdressers, as worthwhile as painting your own nails in advance of an appointment with the beautician, as beneficial as going on a diet before having liposuction. You get the picture. It really is rather pointless to clean your home when you are paying someone else to do it. It's not like anybody's going to judge you on how clean your house is or anything. Oh. Right. I forgot. You're a woman over thirty. Of course you're going to be judged on how clean your house is. Duh!

UNWANTED GUESTS

There's a time like no other when your propensity to be pristine gets out of hand, and this is of course when you have guests to stay. There was something cool when you were younger about having people over, or "sleepovers" as you called them then – a hangover perhaps from the pyjama parties of your (then) recent childhood. So, if Joe Bloggs had a few too many, you'd have been happy to stumble over him in the morning if he'd kipped on your sofa, and it's only when he started to hang around like a bad smell (and he probably did!) for a few days that you'd kick him out.

Indeed, your tolerance towards your guests was quite something, and it would take an act of extreme revolt-ingness for you to kick them out (in most cases you'd usually just kick them into the garden or the cupboard under the stairs until they sobered up).

In a reversal of this open-house policy you'd now rather have unwelcome guests of the creepy-crawly or rodent varieties than have human guests dropping by. Well, almost. In spite of this, if you *must* have family or friends to visit (and let's face it, it's the former you dread the most), you project the outward appearance of appreciating their visit and put on an Oscar-winning act of a warm welcome.

You can be sure you're following in the footsteps of a certain female relative if such visits compel you to re-examine the cleanliness of your home, casting your eye over it as if you were expecting Kim and Aggie themselves to grace you with their presence! Previously unwashed windows are given a once, twice and three times over, cobwebs dusted from the ceiling (well, Uncle Tom is quite tall and you'd just die if he got some dust on his toupee) and the toilet scrubbed, polished and bleached to within an inch of its life. When your visitors arrive you make all the right noises, laying on flowers, guest towels and soaps. You treat your own house, in fact, like a hotel, but live in hope that your guests won't do the same!

But then, after a few days, or even hours or minutes, you crave solitude, peace and quiet and make your way to bed with a migraine. As you do, a light bulb appears above your head and the frequency of your own Mum's migraines is suddenly explained! She couldn't wait to be rid of everyone…

When you take on the role of guest, you are no less agitated. From the outside it would seem that you are simply being helpful, as you offer to bring your own bedding, towels and even dishcloths. But we know better, don't we, ladies? Such is your new-born predilection towards household perfection, you can't bear the thought of sleeping in someone else's dirty sheets! It's likewise obvious why you make yourself available to do the washing-up when visiting the rellies. 1. It gets you out of the living room where Great Uncle Ted has decided to regale his stories of war-time horror for the umpteenth time. (Not that you're unsympathetic but really, was The War that bad for people who lived in the Highlands of Scotland?) 2. It's the only way you can be certain that the crockery and cups are clean enough for your exacting high standards. (Who could blame you? We all know that Great

Uncle Ted likes to annoy you by keeping his false teeth in your coffee cup overnight.) Oh well, never mind, you'll be back home soon enough.

"Darling... after two weeks at your sister's she has finally given us a set of scales."

Now we've been all round the houses, it's time to bed down for the night – in your own home, of course. Where – suffice to say – the bedspread has been turned down, the Teasmade is ready to go in the morning, and a hot water bottle has been filled to keep your tootsies warm. Now what was that rhyme you used to hear at bedtime? "Night, Night, sleep tight, don't let the bed bugs bite." Some chance of that! Your bedclothes are more sterile than a baby's bottle and your nightgown has the "exotic", fresh scent of Lenor. All's going to plan to end the day on the clean and tidy tip on which it started. But what's this? Here comes that great hulk of fur and smells that's bound to ruin your picture of perfection. No, no, not your husband. Let's not be too harsh! I mean, the cat. The only creature in the house who smells, comes home late, doesn't wash and is *still* allowed in your bed!

Chapter 10

Mother Knows Best

Sometimes truths are so eternal that they are best expressed in song, and in this case it's Paul McCartney and *Wings* who can easily do my job for me, with their 1973 song, *Live and Let Die*. Allow me to quote: "When you were young and your heart was an open book, you used to say live and let live…" and when Sir Paul's backing singers warble, "you know you did, you know you did, you know did," they might well be singing directly to you.

Yes, you, a woman who once let people live and let live, let bygones be bygones and other such clichés, and was more likely to turn to people for advice than dish it out herself. You might have pored over self-help books, written to agony aunts or even – in a fit of desperation – used your mother as a confidante. And if things had gone from bad to worse, you'd not have thought twice about seeking professional help. Your therapist was your closest friend and ally!

There comes a time, though, when the tables turn, when you decide that all other advice is not worth the paper it's written on, and you lose grip on all the tips and tricks you've picked up along the years. Why, you think, self-assuredly, surely your own life experience serves you better than relying on other people's guidance? You might call this half a lifetime of acquired knowledge old wives' tales, you might call it good old-fashioned commonsense…

153

Call it what you will, but I'm afraid, the most accurate name for it is received wisdom. And where did you receive this wisdom from? Come on, think now… what's this book all about? That's right! From your Mother. And could this echoing of her wise and well-used words be the truest sign that you are turning into her?

Because there are unlimited occasions when you regurgitate her words. Or rather, we should say, when you projectile vomit her words, as your use of them is both deeply unpleasant and seems to happen against your will! You know the lines I'm talking about here – the ones we've seen throughout the book, the ones you swore would never pass your lips, the ones we've called her classic Mum sayings and expressions.

But it's in the realm of giving out advice that you have really come into her own (yes, your Mum's own, not your own), for you have become expert at doling out these parentally inspired platitudes. Don't deny it! We were all going to wear our hearts on our sleeves about this one, remember? So, come on, reel them out.

BAD OLD-FASHIONED ADVICES

There is no end to the list of subjects on which you now deem yourself an *expert* – or sometimes on which your household expects you to be an expert. Well, you're not going to put them straight are you? It serves you too well to maintain the aura of being the all-seeing, all-knowing one in your clan – it means there's less chance of anybody answering you back! Besides, what are mothers for, if not to be the fountain of all… well, not quite knowledge… but useful information maybe?

But let's admit it. Usually family members, especially the youngsters, don't come *asking* for therapy from Dr Mum. It's just that you can't stop yourself from unlocking your inner Claire Rayner at the drop of a hat!

A key area of your uncalled-for counselling is clothing. And let's be specific about this, we are talking specifically here about something that has been a bone of contention for mothers and daughters the world over since year dot. A thing which mothers everywhere have gone to great lengths (there's a clue here!) to keep down and their daughters have fought to bring back up. No, I'm not talking about your dodgy fish lasagne recipe, I'm referring of course to… hemlines.

Now, if you have settled down to read this book, if you've reached that inescapable stage when life's rich tapestry has started to fray at the edges, then I'm pretty sure you were a teen in the 1970s or '80s – a time when hemlines weren't exactly dropping to the floor in modest and demure folds. Check out your photo albums, and you'll find yourself in a racy '70s micro-mini or hideous '80s puff ball. You might, at the same time, bring to mind the hot-headed rows you had over how much thigh you were showing or how cold you'd get waiting for the bus. (You knew it was worth it though, eh? You were hardly going to pull the local lush wearing trousers or anything that fell below the knee. Besides, you and your gang of gal pals were known as the "leggy lassies" so anything demure just wouldn't do.)

"It's a record of my daughter's rising hemline."

Why is it, then, that you will now use all your matriarchal might and main to stop your own daughter sporting the latest bum-freezing fashions? Why can't you simply bite your tongue, rather than giving her a tongue-lashing, hollering, "You're going out wearing THAT?" and "I've seen page 3 girls more covered up than you are." I'll tell you why, because if she's wearing mini-skirts, then it can mean only one thing. Yes. She has become interested, just like you did, in BOYS.

Uh-oh! It's paranoia aplenty for you from now on! From this moment on you will develop a growing obsession with your daughter's impending love and – dare I say it – sex life, and I'd bet my last dollar you'll think your constant interference in it will make a difference. It won't.

Not content with having taken most of our own teens and twenties to deliberate over our choice of partner, as we turn into our Mums we take it on ourselves to decide who's the best match for our children. Relationships then become a key area for our fault-finding, nit-picking and goat-getting. It's fair to say our approach depends on whether it's our son or daughter who is looking for love. Let's face it, where sons are concerned, the late Princess Di/Kylie Minogue/The Virgin Mary herself could walk through the front door and we'd find fault. As for our daughters, even if the mild-mannered, kindly-faced boy next door came a-knocking, we'd fear his only desire is to get her knocked up!

You may have always said you'd let your kids live their lives as they wish, but the Boy Next Door suddenly appears to be the Molester Next Door, and the Girl Next Door nothing but a scheming tramp. And so you dole out advice and your hard-won-wisdom – and, if you're a modern gal and exceptionally touchy, condoms.

And if the worst comes to the worst (or worst comes to best as you secretly think), and your young gun is dumped, you shamelessly mop up those teenage tears, delighted with the chance to you employ another annoying age-worn expression, to an angst-ridden Fred, Leroy or Shirley, "He/she is not worth 10 of you!"

But if you are world-class at churning out unsolicited advice, you are conversely tight-lipped when people actually approach you with a question! As we've mentioned before, we swerve the question "What's for dinner?" with more skill and dexterity than Lewis Hamilton on a wet race track. Or perhaps the best comparison would be with your own Mum when you ask her a question! Don't you remember her artful way of evading any issue? Similarly, when your nearest and dearest mistake you for a tracking system, for a veritable database of information able to pinpoint the location of every single item they own, you relish the chance to angrily churn out that wonderful old chestnut, "It's where you left it!" (No Mum, it's where YOU left it, if you think back to your special "hiding places".) Yet, it's with the following answer, that we could crown you queen of the comebacks. An answer which can be used to avoid all manner of awkward queries, from "Where do babies come from?" to "What is pocket money?" to the teenage classic, "Can I go to Amy/Juan's for a sleep-over?" It's the secret weapon used by fed-up mothers across the land; that golden oldie: "Ask your father!" Best employed with a surly frown, which says "back off little buddy."

MUM RAGE

Hmm, getting quite a temper, aren't you? No surprise really. It's often said that a hint that you're headed for the crest of the hill (you're not over the hill just yet) is when your tolerance of your fellow human beings wanes; that your new-found dislike of people (for standing in front of you in a queue, parking in your "spot" or simply existing!) is a sign you're becoming the archetypal Grumpy Old Woman... Road rage, for instance, could also suggest that the grey hand of middle age beckons sooner rather than later. (You don't see young women or girl racers getting naffed off in a traffic jam – they just paint their nails and crank up Radio 1 to deafening levels.)

But it's another form of anger which is a better sign that you've been dragged kicking and screaming – and you will be, literally – into your new role as Mum impersonator extraordinaire. This is a blinding-white-lighting-strike of anger that rises up in us unexpectedly at the slightest provocation And that's Mum rage. Your level of Mum rage may vary and depend on several aggravating factors including: numbers of family members living at home or "under your feet'; whether your hormones are playing ball – or playing havoc – that particular day; and just how messy the house is.

Level one Mum rage is a fairly tame affair. Comparable, say, to a slight earth tremor, Richter scale 1, and nothing to get the scientists worked up about. Level one Mum rage might come about if you've called everyone in for tea but 10 minutes later they're still at the computer/in the shed/ having their fourth shower of the day (delete inappropriate teatime activity as appropriate). The physical manifestation of level one Mum rage is a slightly raised temperature, a hot flush and a quick blast of "I'm going to get cross in a minute!" Oh dear… These words are a clear sign that you're actually *already* cross. Best progress to the next level.

As we do so, you may well leave the earth – as well as your family – quaking in your wake. You can expect level two Mum rage to be triggered by some everyday household mishap: if somebody inadvertently sticks in a black sock with the whites wash and everything comes out grey, or if you send someone to the shops for a pint of milk and they come back with a tabloid newspaper, a courgette and packet of crisps. (No prizes for guessing who that might be.) At which point you vibrate with indignation; objects – inanimate or otherwise – might be thrown; and your face takes on a startling resemblance to Edvard Munch's *The Scream*. Albeit a slightly redder version than the original. (Yes, *The Scream*. Don't kid yourself that, with that temper, your visage has the sedate appeal of the *Mona Lisa*.) During level two Mum rage, the family may try to escape to the privacy of their own bedrooms but wood, bricks, mortar and even make-shift locks aren't going to stop you, oh no! You've got a spleen and you're going to vent it. The original misdemeanour which triggered your rage is soon forgotten, but this doesn't stop you getting a whole number of other issues off your chest. Why does everybody need to be told to tidy their things away, why can't they just do it on auto-pilot? Tick! Wouldn't it be nice if just one day somebody else could make dinner without being asked. Tick! Don't stop, you're on a roll…

Better batten down the hatches, then, for the most serious level of Mum rage – level three. Level three Mum rage is usually saved for special occasions – anniversaries, birthdays and, not least, Christmas. Why is it that your kith and kin save their utter disregard for all your hard work, their mind-boggling lack of appreciation for your sterling efforts as matriarch, for these special days? Well, more fool them. For then a year's worth of resentment about smelly socks, inappropriate frocks and squabbling about what to watch on the box builds up and you explode with the violence – and unreliability – of a Christmas cracker. Nobody can guess when and what will finally make you blow!

There's little doubt that you are turning into your Mum when you reach such Vesuvian peaks of Mum rage, and there's none left in your mind at all, as you pack a small suitcase on Christmas morning, slam the front door and yell, "I'm off to my mother's! See you in the New Year!"

THE MARTYRDOM OF MOTHERHOOD

But you'll be back before long, won't you? Because, if you're honest, you revel in the martyrdom of being a Mum, the inches you give, and the miles the family take, the things you've given up to become a mother – err, like nearly everything – and the small gestures you make for your offspring, which they don't even notice (or at least which they pretend not to notice).

Because there's nothing like motherhood to give you an excuse for a good old moan! You'd have given birth years sooner if you'd known what whingeing and fault-finding you could get away with.

And yet you continue to revel in your self-sacrifice on a daily basis. The reason you exaggerate the misery of motherhood is to win accolades, respect... but most of all obedience! It means you can turn around and belt out yet more hand-me-down expressions such as "You lot don't even know you're born" or, "The things I've given up for you kids!" (Even if what you gave up for them was a job you secretly hated, and getting away from a boss you hated even more!)

"I just wish she wouldn't walk us to school."

The climax, the apogee if you will, of milking your status as martyr is Mothering Sunday. This is a day when mothers in the western world are ostensibly meant to be rewarded for the sacrifices they've made – when they're given a pat on the back for putting up with 365 days – less this measly one – of motherhood.

And so, when you wake up on Mother's Day you make the most of it. Not by enjoying breakfast in bed, not by delighting in the bunch of flowers the kids' Dad picked from the back garden moments before you woke up, nor even because you may receive a deeply inappropriate gift, like a compilation of soppy love songs, a fancy oven glove or a "luxury" set of tea towels. (Just because they're fancy doesn't stop them making you feeling dowdy, misunderstood and middle-aged!) No, the real reason you adore Mother's Day is because when you smell the burning toast, hear the shrill cries of rough-play gone wrong or the ambulance pull up the driveway –as Dad tried to usurp your own position – you can crawl out of bed, five minutes into your lie-in, and say, "Ooh, you just can't get along without me, can you?"

And as you do so, you realize with horror how much you have come to emulate her, the great Matriarch, your own Mother. And when, that afternoon of Mothering Sunday, you make the necessary trip to her place, and she winds you up something rotten, you might turn to your husband on the journey home, and say, "Shoot me the day I turn into my Mother." (In fact you keep a loaded pistol in the cupboard under the stairs for this very purpose. Two bullets though. One for you and one in case him indoors should ever turn into his Dad.)

"Say hello to your mother..."

As we finish this chapter and come to the end of this book, it should come as no surprise to you, with what we're learnt along the way, that your husband's response to this is to raise his eyebrows, shrug his shoulders and give you a look that says, "Dear, you already are!" Oh, oh. Well I guess this leaves you with two options. You could go quietly, give in to the inevitable and enjoy the fact that you're turning into your Mum. I mean, it's not so bad, is it? Think of all the effort you'd have to make to avoid maternal mutation – the evidence is plain for all to see inside this book. And it's not like you're turning into your Gran or anything... Alternatively you could assemble every woman in your peer-group, put on your mutton-est clothes, set the radio to 1 Xtra and give the hopeful collective yell, "Help! We're turning into our mothers!" But don't come crying to me when your screams fall on deaf ears. You have been well and truly warned!

Appendix

MUM'S TIMETABLES FOR SOCIAL EVENTS

Dinner Party Countdown

Four weeks before

Choose guests, menu and theme – the latter two being tailored to the first, natch. Send out invites.

Three weeks before

Order meat from butcher, seafood from fishmonger and dessert from the darling little patisserie in town.

Two weeks before

Panic. Nobody has replied. Do they all hate you? Nope, but they are probably thinking, "get a life" after seeing your premature invitation.

One week before

Clean the house from top to bottom, even rooms you don't think your guests will enter. Scratch that. Especially the rooms you don't think your guests will enter. Sod's law, these will be the ones they want to nose around in.

Evening before

Polish cutlery, lay table, iron outfit, get make-up and accessories ready. Don't sleep a wink.

Morning of the big night

Go to the loo several times. Panic-buy a second dessert and some nibbles, as well as three further bottles of wine.

Lunchtime

Go to bed with blinding migraine, overcome with the task you've set yourself. I mean, a poussin inside a chicken inside a capon? Whatever was I thinking?

"Tea minus one hour thirty minutes and ten seconds."

Two hours before

Wake up and yell at husband who has let you sleep for hours. Come downstairs to find he's stuffed the chicken and left the other fowl in the fridge. Consider divorce at the shame of offering a simple chicken for dinner.

Five minutes before

Put on some lippy, neck a litre of vodka and swear you'll never be hosting a dinner party again! And the festivities haven't even begun!

Christmas Countdown

10. Boxing Day (we're talking about the Boxing Day BEFORE the following Christmas here)

Buy as many Christmas-themed items in the sales as possible – the cheaper, the better. Half-bashed-in baubles, torn wrapping paper, tangled tinsel – you'll find a use for all of them next year.

9. Summer prior to Christmas

Be sure to keep an eye out for appropriate Christmas presents on your summer holidays. Never know what stunning local artefacts you could pick up for aunt Flossie along the way. She always did have a penchant for pottery.

8. Early September

Make Christmas cake and mince pies.

"Just because I don't want to start Xmas
Shopping in October."

7. Late September

Panic as you've not yet written your Christmas present list. Write list (forgetting items stashed away in the cupboard after your summer holiday).

6. October

Send cards to foreign relatives to make sure they arrive on time. Duh! Post only takes a week or so to the continent. Oh well, better to be safe than sorry. Do lion's share of Christmas shopping.

5. November

Send remaining Xmas cards, wrap all presents, dig out Christmas decorations from the loft.

4. Early to mid-December

Instil rising sense of panic in other family members as you smugly say, "Well, I've been done with my Christmas shopping for weeks."

3. Christmas Eve

Par-boil potatoes, peel sprouts, drink wine, make stuffing, put the kids to bed with a healthy dose of Medised, drink more wine, weep over midnight mass on the radio. Stumble into bed.

2. Christmas morning – 3am

Wake with a start upon realization that you've not taken a bite from Santa's mince pie or half-munched Rudolph's carrot. My God! Little Jimmy (who can't even SAY Santa) will be sure to cotton on that you're a big fat LIAR. Pad downstairs to find husband still frantically wrapping presents. That toaster better not be for you!

1. Christmas morning – actual morning

Get up before everybody else and hoover and polish to make sure everything is "just perfect". Help yourself to a wee G&T. The first of many!

Quiz

ARE YOU TURNING INTO YOUR MUM?

There should be little doubt left in your mind whether you are turning into your Mum. And if you can't remember what you've read, there is a high chance that, yes, you are headed down that long road to Mum-land. But just in case you need some help deciding at the final hurdle, here's a small test to make things crystal clear:

1. The last thing you read was

a) The back of a cereal packet: why read when you can partay?

b) *More* magazine's "position of the week" feature. Well, you looked at the pictures anyway;

c) A devastatingly beautiful piece of fiction, specially selected for your book group, thanks to Richard and Judy's book club.

2. The concept "going green" means the following to you

a) Something you do after a few too many lager shandies;

b) Making a token effort to recycle the many wine bottles piling up in my back yard;

c) It's your life, the universe and everything.

3. Complete this phrase. "Men are good for nothing except..."

a) Sex;

b) Presents and sex, in no particular order;

c) Fixing stuff, presents and sex – in that order.

4. And this one. "I shop till I..."

a) Drop my first "e" of the evening, then I hit the clubs instead;

b) Drop my wallet on the floor. But then I just use the plastic;

c) Drop my computer mouse on the floor. I only buy online these days.

5. Your favourite Victorian style icon is

a) Victoria Beckham – I'd do anything to look like Posh!

b) Victoria's Secret – good underwear covers up your increasing midriff;

c) Queen Victoria – respectable and long skirts are the name of the game these days.

6. If awake at 4am you would be

a) About to hit the after-club party;

b) Rising so I arrive bright and early at my fantastic new job;

c) Unsurprised. What with stress, snoring and your son, it'd be a wonder if you were ever asleep at this hour.

7. You have five quid left in your purse until payday. You spend it on

a) Entry to a bar – you won't need more than that as you'll be shouted drinks all night;

b) A bottle of wine, with enough left over for your fare to work tomorrow;

c) The evening meal, a pair of new knickers, and a bottle of plonk. And you've fifty pence left over. Don't you just love Aldi?

8. "Neighbours, everybody needs…"

a) Cool neighbours. Especially the ones who sell weed;

b) Quiet neighbours who are a little hard of hearing. After all, you might want to throw the occasional party;

c) Watchful neighbours, so long as they remember not to knock after 8pm.

9. How many hours a week do you spend doing housework?

a) If you call listening to "house music" doing housework, I'm at it 24/7;

b) An hour here and there, unless my Mother is coming to visit, then you can double it;

c) Hours? Don't insult me. How many days do I spend, more like. Oh, and the answer is about five…

10. "Mother knows…"

a) Sod all. Interfering old witch is always trying to tell me what to do;

b) More than I'll ever let on;

c) Best. Whatever else?

See how you scored on page 182.

The Mum-o-meter

If you answered mostly As: you're reading this book as some kind of joke, right? You're about as close to turning into your Mum as I am to being a teenager. Yup, those teenage years are a dim and distant memory for me, and your future role as your Mum should be far off in the future. Lucky you!

If you answered mostly Bs: unlike Mrs Thatcher, the lady is for turning. Into your Mum, in this case. Come on, if you're old enough to remember *her*, you're more than well on your way. Mind you, there's life in you yet, but you're not the rock 'n' roll rebel you once were, missy, so don't give me that look!

If you answered mostly Cs: congratulations. Let me rephrase that – commiserations! You *are* turning into your Mum. Sorry.

Glossary

MUM-SPEAK

Do you speak Mum? Or would you like to learn the lingo? Below you'll find a few catchphrases which may remind you of your own childhood days or help you down that long road to Mums-ville. Wait – what am I talking about? You don't need my help where that's concerned!

"Ask your father"

The time-worn tool used by Mums everywhere to bat those especially awkward questions to the man of the house. Particularly useful for all matters financial, biological and sexual.

"Beer before wine, you'll feel fine; wine before beer, you'll feel queer"

A phrase best used late in the evening when you've already had wine, then beer, beer, than wine, and er, which way

"It's a little read book... the sayings of charwoman mum."

round was it? And which way round does that saying go again? Time, and your hangover, will tell.

"Because I said so"
The killer come-back to the ubiquitous question, "WHY?"

"Cheap at half the price"
A statement so illogical that only someone on the road to maternal emulation would use it.

"Do what you think is best"
A very useful cop-out phrase when the questioner's dilemma is so tricky that you can't come up with a decent answer, or so banal that you couldn't give a monkey's what they do.

"I can't even hear myself think"
Best yelled at a hundred decibels during an argument where ironically enough you've been the one doing all the shouting. No wonder you can't hear yourself think.

"If your friend jumped off a cliff, would you do the same?"

Something you say when your children are copying their friends to the same degree as you're copying your Mum. (But you're possibly crossing your fingers at the same time that they do take a running jump.)

"I'm bound to say"

What follows, like the phrase itself, is something extremely predictable and Mum-like, e.g., "I'm bound to say, that skirt could do with being a few inches longer."

"It'll all come out in the wash"

The kind of nonsensical platitude that only you and your Mum still use. I mean, it doesn't all come out in the wash.

"I want doesn't get"

Sure it doesn't. Even after it has been repeated *ad nauseam* while you're trying to settle down to *Woman's Hour*?

"Look after the pennies, the pounds will take after themselves"

Another saying which shows your age. I mean, it's not like anyone keeps pennies in their piggy-bank anymore, is it? Fivers and tenners are where it's at these days.

"Send us a postcard"

The phrase that confirms beyond all others that you are just sooo last century. Never heard of texting or email? As for social networking sites like Facebook or MySpace, you run a mile. Something which connects you more to the people around you? You do your utmost to avoid most people, thank you very much!

"Shoot me when I turn into my Mum"

The Mother of all Mums' sayings which should leave you in no doubt that your maternal mutation is all but complete. This statement invariably brings only one response: raised eyebrows and a smirk which says, "I think you already have."

"Tell the truth and shame the devil"

Yeah, and if you think that attempt to worm the truth out of them is going to work in this day and age, you're either (1) mad, (2) extremely religious or (3) turning into your Mum.

"To fail to prepare is to prepare to fail"

Ever so "useful" when said to your partner the day before he attends an interview that he has put off dealing with, or to teenage children the day before an exam.

"Think before you speak"

You should know by now this is going to lead to some smart-arse reply with the scientific explanation that it's humanly impossible NOT to think before you speak.

"Where you left it!"

This is about as helpful as you get when you are displaying the first symptoms of Mum rage.

"Whining doubles the job"

An unusually accurate one this, and perhaps more annoying (and effective) than the similar "A smile costs less than a frown" for this reason. Take note!

"What do you take me for – a taxi service?!"

Even funnier if nosiness or paranoia means it was you who insisted on picking up your passenger in the first place! True, Winchester can be pretty scary of an evening.

"When I was your age"

When you were *their* age, you did and said exactly what they are doing and saying to you now. And now you're *your* age, you do and say exactly the same thing as your Mum. Ah! How reassuring that the wheel of life keeps turning!

"Would you like some cheese with that whine?"

Spare our aching sides! It's a pun a minute with you around. (Note we said pun, not laugh, a minute.)

"You can't have your cake and eat it"

It's an old but gold saying, highly effective when you want to deflect pester power and demands for the latest gadget or gizmo… and that's just from your husband!

"I've turned into my mother."